The Touch of Truth

A Novel by

Sharad Ganpatye

AF517074

Published by Sharad Ganpatye

A Copyright Notice

The Touch of Truth

© 2025 Sharad Ganpatye

All rights reserved

No part of this book may be copied, stored, adapted into a movie/series or shared in any form—print or digital—without written permission from the author.

You are most welcome to quote brief passages for reviews, articles, or personal reflections, provided proper credit is given.

ISBN: ISBN: 9789334406757

This is a work of fiction. Names, characters, organizations, places, events, and incidents are either the products of the author's imagination or are used fictitiously. Any resemblance to actual persons, living or dead, or to actual organizations, whether operating or defunct, or to actual events is purely coincidental.

First Edition –Oct 2025

Published by **Sharad Ganpatye**

Mumbai, India

FOREWORD

By Former Justice **Pramod Kode**,
High Court of Judicature at Bombay

Criminal trials are voyages in quest of truth, revealing the struggle between the light and dark sides of mankind. The judge, the aggrieved/aggressor, and all others involved in the courtroom process witness a rainbow of emotions from dozens of people in the legal profession.

The novel *The Touch of Truth* by Sharad Ganpatye from my hometown of Thane stirred in me an array of emotions. This novel is not just a fictional story but unfolds the journey of a man set to prove his innocence and how a simple human becomes powerful in the toughest wars faced to safeguard his own reputation.

The protagonist, Ajay Sharma, an IIT gold medallist, chooses the job of teaching over a corporate career. This struck me as a great quality in the protagonist, as he lived his life to enlighten and inspire students as opposed to just choosing luxuries with a big fat corporate pay cheque.

Though we see Ajay facing tragedies in life—the worst being the loss of his young daughter and later the collapse of his marriage—yet he didn't falter and kept going in life.

He filled the empty space of his heart with his adopted daughter Pallavi. Even while he sips a cup of tea as she observes the world with wide-eyed wonder, her presence makes the cracks of his heart heal.

As a person ages, he becomes more responsible, emotional, and mature. However, even before Ajay took on the responsibility of marriage and parented his daughter, as a student, he helped expose a child trafficking racket, rescuing many children and guiding them towards dignity and success.

But as good people are always tested the most, his good acts of helping people later were turned into accusations which in turn threatened his honour.

They say, "You're a reflection of what you put out to the world," and thus the testimony of six women, rescued years ago by our protagonist, proved this.

The novel takes us perfectly through the pain of false accusations, the injustice of media trials, and the isolation of a man under suspicion. At the same time, it also shows us how loyalty plays the biggest role in winning at life, as when the protagonist's estranged wife Nandini returns to support him. The protagonist's father has never been a man of many words, but he has always stood as a pillar protecting his son, and his belief in this challenging time makes all the difference in the world to him.

Facing a problem, hardship, tragedy, etc., and coming out of it gives a person a second lease on life. Thus, after his acquittal, the protagonist and his family live a life focused on public service and building the nation.

Through Ajay's journey, the author Mr. Sharad Ganpatye reminds us of these timeless truths:

- Children, no matter where they come from, are valued and deserve to live with respect.
- Truth never stays in the dark; it may take time, but the truth will always come out.
- Kindness, compassion, and humanity are the backbone of our society, and helping those in need gives us our Utopia on this Earth.
- Karma always serves you what you served others; hence no good deed is wasted.

Having spent four decades in industry—working with diverse molecules and safeguarding lives—Mr. Ganpatye, a chemical engineer by training, now safeguards values in society through his writing, with the precision of an engineer and the heart of a humanist. His "small world," as he calls it, has given birth to a story the larger world must embrace.

I wish Sharad Ganpatye the very best on his literary journey and appeal to you, the reader: read stories but apply the lessons learned from them in your life too.

Stand by those who need support. Give people a chance and believe in their truth. If you do, *The Touch of Truth* will not merely remain a novel you have read—it will become a truth you have lived and honoured.

Pramod Kode

Former Justice
High Court of Judicature at Bombay

Author's Note

The Touch of Truth is a work of fiction born from deep reflection on real-world injustices, human resilience, and the transformative power of compassion.

While the characters, events, institutions, and locations in this novel are entirely imaginary, the emotions, dilemmas, and social realities they represent are very much part of our world. This story is not based on any specific case, but it is inspired by the quiet battles fought in classrooms, courtrooms, and homes—battles of character and courage.

Through Ajay Sharma and the lives he touches, I have attempted to explore the fragility of reputation, the burden of false accusations, the healing strength of mentorship, and the extraordinary light that even the most wounded souls can carry forward. My hope is that readers will not only follow Ajay's journey but also pause to reflect on the way we, as a society, respond to scandal, suspicion, and silence.

Writing a novel is never a solitary act, even when most of the work happens in quiet hours. I am deeply grateful to my family for their unwavering support, especially during the times when this story consumed my days and nights. My sincere thanks also go to the Honourable Mr. Pramod Kode, former Justice, High Court of Judicature at Bombay, for his thoughtful and generous foreword. His distinguished perspective brings invaluable weight and insight to this work. If this book stirs even one reader to look at such situations with greater empathy and critical thought, I will consider my work worthwhile.

I dedicate this book to every teacher who stood firm, every child who waited to be seen, and every parent who believes in nurturing their child with love and values. This is for the truths that trembled but survived.

Sharad Ganpatye, Thane, Maharashtra, India 2025

The Table of Content

Chapter 1: From Corner Room to Classroom 1

Morning Ritual

Chapter 2: The Accusation 33

A touch Misunderstood

Chapter 3: Shadows of the Past 57

From Teacher to Suspect

Chapter 4: The Fire Spreads 85

The Court of Public Opinion

Chapter 5: Echoes in Courtroom 113

The Arena of Truth

Chapter 6: The Verdict 155

The Hour of Truth

Chapter 7: Return of the Teacher 171

Back Where He Belonged

Chapter 8: Lessons Beyond the Classroom 183

From Vision to Realty

Chapter 9: A Gathering of Hope 193

A Decade of Transformation

Chapter 1: From Corner Room to Classroom

Morning Ritual

Ajay Sharma stood at the narrow balcony of his modest apartment in Pune, a cup of tea warming his hands as the chilly morning breeze brushed against his skin. The ceramic mug, chipped at the rim from years of faithful service, held more than just tea- it cradled his daily ritual of reflection. The sky was tinged with hues of orange and lavender, painting the horizon like water colours bleeding into wet paper. Below, the city was slowly stirring to life, emerging from its nocturnal slumber with the reluctant grace of a sleepy giant.

Beside him, on a small plastic chair that perfectly fit her six-year-old frame, sat Pallavi. Her dark hair was still tousled from sleep, and she wore her favourite purple pyjamas with tiny stars scattered across the fabric like wishes waiting to be made. In her small hands, she carefully held her own cup- a miniature version of her father's, filled with warm milk sweetened with just a touch of honey. Her legs swung gently back and forth, too short to reach the ground, creating a soft rhythm that matched the peaceful morning tempo.

School buses honked through the narrow lanes with their familiar urgency, parents waved hurried goodbyes from doorways and balconies, their voices carrying traces of both love and the day's mounting anxieties, and children with oversized backpacks ran clumsily toward their stops, their laughter piercing the morning air like scattered notes of a joyful symphony. A few street vendors were already setting up their carts with practiced efficiency, the metallic clang of their equipment creating a rhythmic backdrop as they prepared for another day in the fast-beating heart of the city.

From the balcony, Ajay watched it all quietly, as he did every morning, his eyes taking in the familiar choreography of urban life unfolding below. The stillness in his dark eyes wasn't apathy- it was a mindful pause before another purposeful day, a moment of centring that had become as essential to him as breathing. The fragrance of his lightly brewed cardamom tea, with its warm, earthy notes, reminded him that life, despite its inevitable bitterness, had its sweet and grounding moments that could anchor a soul even in the stormiest of times.

Pallavi observed the world below with the wide-eyed wonder that only children possess. Her small fingers traced patterns on the condensation of her milk cup as she watched a particularly interesting pigeon strutting across the neighbouring rooftop. To her, every morning was an adventure waiting to unfold- the bus driver who always waved at her, the flower vendor who saved the prettiest marigolds for her weekly purchase, the stray cat who had learned to expect her gentle whispers and occasional treats. Her world was painted in bright colours and simple joys, unmarked by the complexities that shadowed adult perspectives.

"Daddy," she said softly, her voice carrying the sleepy sweetness of someone still transitioning from dreams to reality, "do you think the birds know we're watching them?"

Ajay smiled, his heart swelling with the kind of pure love that only a father could understand. "What do you think, beta?"

She tilted her head thoughtfully, a gesture she had inherited from him, though she was unaware of the resemblance. "I think they do. See how that one keeps looking at us?" She pointed to a small sparrow perched on the ledge, its head cocked curiously in their direction.

"Maybe he's wondering what we're thinking about," Ajay

suggested, delighting in her innocent observations.

"I'm thinking about my drawing for art class today," Pallavi announced with the seriousness that children reserve for their most important projects. "I want to draw our morning tea time. You with your big cup and me with my little one."

His balcony, though small and cramped by most standards, had become their retreat- a sacred space they shared each morning before the world called them to their respective duties. It was their launch pad before he walked into his chosen battlefield armed with nothing but compassion and unwavering determination, and before she skipped into her classroom armed with crayons, curiosity, and an unshakeable belief that every day held magic.

For many bustling past on the street below, this was just another weekday, another step in the endless march of routine. But for Ajay, every day at Vidya Vihar High School was a mission, a calling that resonated in his bones. A silent campaign to change what truly mattered- not in the headlines that screamed for attention, not in the boardrooms where profits were calculated, but in the minds of small children learning how to spell "hope," their innocent voices turning letters into dreams.

For Pallavi, now in her third year at the same school after being adopted at three and admitted to Jr. KG at four, every day was an expedition into a world of discovery. She loved the way simple sentences came together during language class, how she could now read small stories during reading hours, and how she could write her name in neat letters during writing practice. But most of all, she loved knowing that her Daddy was just a few classrooms away, teaching children the same age as her in Standard 1B with the same patience and kindness he showed her every morning over their shared tea and milk.

He was an unlikely figure in the kindergarten corridors, his tall frame and thoughtful demeanour standing out among the colourful chaos of tiny chairs and finger-painted walls. An IIT gold medallist in MTech, Ajay had stunned his professors and peers alike when he chose not to pursue a high-paying corporate job that would have guaranteed him a corner office and a six-figure salary. After two years in the tech world, where he had excelled but felt spiritually empty, he walked away from corner offices and bonus cheques to take a teaching job- one that paid a fraction but filled a deeper void within him that money could never touch.

She was an equally unlikely figure among the children of affluent families who populated the school's junior wing- a child who had known abandonment and hunger before she had known unconditional love and security. But now, at six, she moved through her world with the confidence of someone who had never doubted her worth, never questioned her place in her father's heart, never wondered if she truly belonged. Her laughter rang as freely as any child born to privilege; her dreams stretched as wide as any peer who had never known want.

As the morning sun climbed higher, painting their small balcony in golden light, both father and daughter finished their respective drinks in comfortable silence. Soon, they would walk hand in hand to school—he to teach eager six-year-olds in Standard 1B, while she to learn writing letters and reading simple words in Standard 1C. But for now, in this perfect pocket of peace, they simply existed together, watching the world wake up around them.

"Ready for another adventure, beta?" Ajay asked, standing and extending his hand to her.

Pallavi jumped up with the boundless energy that seemed to refuel itself overnight, placing her small hand in his larger one with complete trust. "Ready, Daddy! Today is going to be a good day."

He squeezed her hand gently, unaware that these would be their last moments of such innocent certainty, their final morning ritual before the storm that would test everything they had built together.

"Yes," he agreed, his voice warm with love and hope. "Today is going to be a very good day."

Together, they stepped back into their apartment, preparing for a day that would begin like any other but would end with their lives forever changed. The balcony stood empty behind them, holding only the lingering warmth of their shared presence and the echo of a little girl's absolute faith that every day held the promise of magic.

The Corporate Years

Those two years in the corporate world had been transformative in ways he hadn't initially anticipated. At Luminflux Solutions, a mid-tier software company with ambitious growth plans, Ajay had quickly distinguished himself not just as a skilled engineer but as someone who understood the intricate dance between innovation and business viability. He possessed that rare combination of technical brilliance and commercial acumen that made him invaluable to the company's expansion strategies.

His colleagues marvelled at his ability to translate complex technical concepts into language that clients could understand, to identify market opportunities that others missed, to develop solutions that were both elegant and profitable.

But it was his natural gift for recognizing and nurturing ideas that truly set him apart. Ajay had an intuitive understanding of what would work in the cutthroat world of technology business—which innovations would capture market attention, which partnerships would yield mutual benefits, which strategies would ensure sustainable growth. He could look at a half-formed concept and see its potential, could take a struggling project and identify the exact adjustments needed to make it succeed.

His ideas didn't just solve problems; they created opportunities, opened new revenue streams, positioned the company ahead of competitors who were still thinking in yesterday's terms.

During his time at Luminflux, Ajay had been responsible for at least three major breakthrough strategies that had significantly boosted the company's market position. His approach to business development was methodical yet creative, combining rigorous analysis with innovative thinking. He understood that in the modern business landscape, success wasn't just about having the best product—it was about understanding your market, anticipating changes, building relationships, and maintaining the agility to adapt when circumstances shifted.

The Secret Arrangement

Ajay's commitment to his chosen path of teaching didn't mean he had abandoned his father's business interests. On the contrary, he had devised an ingenious arrangement that allowed him to support his family's industrial ventures while maintaining his professional independence. Understanding that direct involvement would lead to uncomfortable questions and potential conflicts with his teaching career, he had carefully orchestrated a subtle but effective system of support.

Through a trusted colleague from his corporate days, Ajay had arranged for a business development advisor to work with his father's company. To Abhishek Sharma, this advisor—a seasoned professional named Mr. Raghavan—appeared to be an independent consultant who had approached the company with impressive credentials and innovative ideas. What Abhishek didn't know was that behind Mr. Raghavan's insights lay the strategic mind of his eldest son.

Every week, Ajay spent precisely one hour with Mr. Raghavan, usually over coffee at a small café halfway between his school and his father's factory. These meetings were disguised as casual encounters between old colleagues, but they served a much more significant purpose. During these sessions, Ajay would brief Mr.

Raghavan on market trends he had observed, strategic opportunities he had identified, and specific recommendations tailored to his father's business context.

His understanding of the industry, combined with his knowledge of his father's company's strengths and weaknesses, allowed him to provide insights that were both innovative and practical.

The arrangement was seamless and effective. Mr. Raghavan would present Ajay's ideas to Abhishek as his own professional recommendations, backed by market research and analysis that Ajay had prepared. To ensure authenticity, Ajay even helped Mr. Raghavan develop a network of contacts and resources that would support his credibility as an independent consultant. The result was a steady stream of valuable business advice that helped Abhishek's company navigate challenges, identify new opportunities, and maintain its competitive edge in an increasingly complex market.

Ajay had been careful to ensure that his recommendations were always sound and beneficial. He wasn't just providing ideas; he was taking responsibility for the growth and success of his father's business. When a particular strategy didn't yield expected results, he would work with Mr. Raghavan to adjust the approach, always ensuring that the solutions were practical and achievable. His deep understanding of his father's business philosophy and operational capabilities allowed him to suggest improvements that felt natural and achievable rather than disruptive.

The financial benefits of this arrangement were evident. Under Mr. Raghavan's guidance—which was really Ajay's strategic direction—the company had expanded into two new market segments, streamlined its operations to reduce costs by fifteen percent, and established partnerships that had increased its revenue by nearly thirty percent over the past three years. Abhishek frequently praised Mr. Raghavan's insights, unaware that he was actually benefiting from his son's expertise and love.

For Ajay, this arrangement provided a way to honour his family obligations while maintaining his chosen path. He could contribute to his father's success without compromising his own values or career choices. The weekly meetings with Mr. Raghavan became a bridge between his two worlds—the world of business strategy and growth that he understood intimately, and the world of education and child development that he had chosen to inhabit.

This system also allowed Ajay to maintain his relationship with his father on more neutral ground. When they met at family gatherings, Abhishek would often share his excitement about the business's progress, unknowingly praising the very son whose career choices he had criticized. There was a bittersweet satisfaction in these moments for Ajay—the knowledge that he was supporting his father's dreams even as his father struggled to understand his own.

The arrangement had been running smoothly for more than a decade, and Ajay took quiet pride in the fact that his business acumen was contributing to his family's prosperity. He had found a way to use his skills for both personal fulfilment and family support, proving that success didn't always require choosing between competing loyalties. His strategic mind, honed during his corporate years, had found a new application—not just in building his own career, but in supporting the people he loved while staying true to his chosen path.

Family Disappointment

His professors had warned him that idealism fades fast, their voices heavy with the cynicism of those who had watched too many bright minds surrender to practical concerns, but Ajay's convictions were made of something sturdier than youth. He believed with every fibre of his being that the foundation of a person's life is built before they even know what a resume is, shaped in those tender years when wonder still lives in wide eyes and possibilities seem endless.

He had lied on his resume, a decision that still occasionally pricked at his conscience, submitting only his Higher Secondary Certificate and carefully omitting the prestigious credentials that would have raised uncomfortable questions. The school never questioned him, their administrative staff too overwhelmed and perhaps too grateful to find more than a capable candidate. Why would they probe deeper? A modest, well-spoken young man with a heart-warming smile and a genuine passion for children was a perfect fit for the kindergarten wing, a rare find in a profession that struggled to attract quality educators.

But this decision had come at a price that cut deeper than any financial sacrifice. His parents, Abhishek and Amruta Sharma, were devastated, their dreams for their eldest son crumbling like sandcastles before an unexpected wave. They had raised their son with dreams of prestige and fortune, investing not just money but their hopes and social standing in his education.

His father, an industrialist with roots in engineering and business, a man who had built his reputation on practical success and measurable achievements, couldn't make peace with his son's defiance of the "normal route." The disappointment in Abhishek's eyes was a wound that never quite healed, visible every time they met, every time the conversation turned to careers and futures.

His mother, Amruta, tried to be gentle, her maternal instincts warring with her social anxieties, but her eyes betrayed her silent disappointment, the weight of neighbours' questions and relatives' whispered judgments evident in the way she avoided discussing her son's work at social gatherings.

His younger siblings, Dhanush and Gayatri, supported him emotionally with the fierce loyalty that only siblings can provide, but even they struggled to understand why their brilliant brother had chosen this unconventional life when the world had been his oyster.

Festive gatherings grew quieter, conversations colder, the easy warmth of family slowly replaced by a polite distance that spoke volumes about dreams deferred and expectations shattered.

Love and Partnership

Then there was Nandini Deshmukh, a name that still had the power to make his heart skip a beat even years later.

Nandini, his equal in every sense—an MTech postgraduate from IIT, a vibrant, sharp, driven woman whose intelligence sparkled in her eyes and whose laughter could light up the dreariest of lecture halls. She had fallen in love with Ajay during the quiet hours of project discussions and campus strolls, drawn to his thoughtful nature and the way he listened not just to her words but to the dreams behind them.

Together, they had imagined a future where intellect and idealism coexisted, where success could be measured not just in rupees but in lives touched and minds awakened. Unlike others who questioned his decision with raised eyebrows and sceptical expressions, she admired his courage, saw in his choice a nobility that others missed. Or at least, she once did.

She had held his hand during those uncertain early days and told him, her voice filled with conviction, "Ajay, the world needs more teachers like you. I believe in you." Those words had been his anchor, his source of strength when doubt crept in during sleepless nights.

The Transformative Incident

During their final year at IIT, Ajay and Nandini frequently travelled between their college campus in Mumbai and their hometown of Pune. It was during one such journey that an incident occurred which would profoundly shape Ajay's understanding of his life's purpose.

They had stopped at a roadside tea stall, seeking relief from the sweltering afternoon heat and stretching their legs after hours of driving. As Nandini sipped her tea, savouring the sweet, spiced brew that reminded her of home, she noticed a teenage girl sitting alone near the restaurant entrance. The girl couldn't have been more than fifteen, her clothes threadbare and dirty, her face gaunt with the unmistakable signs of prolonged hunger. Her eyes held a hollow desperation that spoke of days without adequate food, and her frail frame seemed to sway with exhaustion even as she sat motionless on the ground.

"Ajay," Nandini whispered, her voice thick with concern as she gently touched his arm. "Look at that girl. She looks so weak, like she hasn't eaten properly in days."

Ajay's eyes followed Nandini's gaze, and his heart clenched at the sight. Without hesitation, he stood up and approached the girl, his movements gentle and non-threatening. He purchased a packet of biscuits and a bottle of water from the nearby shop, kneeling down to her level as he offered them with a warm smile.

The girl looked up at him with surprise, as if kindness from strangers was a language she had forgotten how to understand. She accepted the food gratefully, her hands trembling slightly as she tore open the packet with the desperate efficiency of someone who had learned not to waste a single morsel.

Throughout the remainder of their drive back to Pune, Ajay remained unusually quiet, his usual animated conversations replaced by a contemplative silence that worried Nandini. She could see the distress in his eyes, the way his jaw tightened whenever he stared out the car window, lost in thoughts that seemed to pain him.

"We should go back tomorrow," he said suddenly, his voice barely audible above the hum of the engine. "We should check on her, make sure she's alright."

The next morning, true to his word, Ajay convinced Nandini to accompany him back to the same tea stall. They searched the area thoroughly, asking vendors and shopkeepers about the girl, but she was nowhere to be found. Their inquiries led them to a devastating discovery—the girl had been struck by a speeding truck the previous evening while crossing the road, and she had died instantly. The news hit them like a physical blow, the senseless tragedy of a young life cut short by circumstances beyond her control leaving them both speechless with grief.

In that moment of shared sorrow and resolve, they found their hands intertwined, each drawing strength from the other's presence. Ajay stated, "In my early college years, I assisted several children experiencing poverty and hardship. They now reside comfortably in a government shelter. She, too, could have benefited from this opportunity." The tragedy had crystallized something within them both, transforming their romantic love into something deeper—a partnership built on common purpose and mutual support. They understood that their privileged education and comfortable backgrounds came with responsibilities, that their love for each other could become a force for loving others who desperately needed it.

The girl's death had not been in vain if it could inspire them to prevent other such tragedies, to ensure that other children wouldn't have to face the world alone and hungry.

Marriage and New Beginnings

They married in a small courtroom ceremony, their union blessed not by elaborate rituals but by the quiet intensity of their shared conviction. No garlands draped with jasmine and roses, no sacred fires witnessed by hundreds of guests, no elders chanting Sanskrit verses that echoed through ornate halls. Just them, their unwavering belief in each other, and the silent rebellion they carried against a world that measured worth in titles and bank balances.

Their eyes spoke of hope and defiance, even as the world around them refused to understand their choice to prioritize love over luxury, meaning over money. Nandini's mother, Sarita Deshmukh, cut ties with her in a dramatic gesture that would have been theatrical if it hadn't been so devastating, their pride wounded by what they saw as their daughter's catastrophic decision.

Her younger sister, Natasha, made it clear with cold, cutting words that Nandini's choice had brought shame upon the family name, that she had destroyed not just her own prospects but tainted the entire lineage. Not a single congratulatory message came from extended family or family friends, their silence more deafening than any harsh words could have been. But the silence only made their bond stronger, forging them into a unit that could weather any storm.

They returned home not to a shower of flowers and celebratory music, but to the flickering light of a single diya (oil lamp) Ajay had lit in their modest kitchen, the tiny flame dancing bravely against the darkness. Nandini changed into a soft cotton saree, the simple fabric more beautiful on her than any silk or designer wear, while Ajay, still in his formal shirt but with his tie loosened and sleeves rolled up, prepared a simple meal of pulao and curd with the careful attention of someone creating a feast.

They ate cross-legged on the floor, their voices soft and intimate, laughing gently at how quietly their lives had changed, how their rebellion had culminated not in grand gestures but in this perfect moment of domestic bliss. That night, with no music but the breeze outside the window and the distant sounds of the city settling into sleep, they danced—awkwardly, joyfully, like children discovering movement for the first time, their shadows swaying against the walls in a private celebration that needed no witnesses.

The Mahabaleshwar Sojourn

That weekend, they took a short trip to Mahabaleshwar, a sleepy hill station where the air was cool and clean, filled with the scent of eucalyptus and the promise of strawberries fresh from the farms. They stayed in a humble guesthouse called "Valley View," with wooden floors that creaked companionably under their feet and foggy windows that turned the world outside into an impressionist painting.

The owner, an elderly Parsi gentleman named Mr. Mehta, greeted them with warm tea and homemade cake, his eyes twinkling with the wisdom of someone who had seen many young couples begin their journey together.

"First time to Mahabaleshwar?" he asked, his voice carrying the gentle accent of his community.

"Yes, sir," Ajay replied, his arm naturally finding its way around Nandini's waist as they stood in the small reception area adorned with faded photographs of the hill station from decades past.

"Ah, perfect weather for romance," Mr. Mehta chuckled, handing them an old-fashioned brass key. "Room 7, second floor. The sunrise view is spectacular from your balcony."

Their room was simple but charming, with a large bed covered in a hand-woven quilt that smelled faintly of lavender and mothballs. The wooden furniture was sturdy and well-worn, speaking of countless other couples who had found refuge here from the world below. A small balcony overlooked the valley, where morning mist danced between the hills like shy spirits playing hide and seek.

That first evening, they walked hand in hand through the narrow lanes of the old bazaar, where vendors sold everything from fresh strawberries to handknitted sweaters. Nandini stopped at a small shop selling local jewellery, her eyes drawn to a simple silver bracelet with tiny bells that chimed softly when she moved her wrist.

"It's beautiful," she said, holding it up to catch the light of the setting sun.

Ajay reached for his wallet, but she stopped him with a gentle touch. "No, let me buy it. A reminder of this moment, of us choosing each other despite everything."

As she fastened the bracelet around her wrist, the tiny bells creating a melodious whisper, Ajay felt a surge of love so powerful it almost brought tears to his eyes. Here was this brilliant, accomplished woman who could have chosen any life, any man, and she had chosen him, chosen this simple existence, chosen love over luxury.

They found a small restaurant tucked away in a corner, its windows glowing warmly against the growing darkness. The owner, a jovial Maharashtrian man with a magnificent moustache, recommended the local specialty—corn bhel and hot chocolate. They sat by the window, watching the lights of the valley twinkle like earthbound stars, their conversation flowing as naturally as the streams that carved the hillsides.

"Do you ever regret it?" Nandini asked suddenly, her fingers tracing patterns on the condensation of her hot chocolate mug.

"Regret what?"

"Choosing this path. Walking away from everything that was expected of us."

Ajay reached across the small table and took her hand, his thumb gently stroking her knuckles. "Never. Not for a single moment. You know why?"

She shook her head, her eyes reflecting the dancing candlelight.

"Because I've learned that success isn't about impressing other people. It's about being able to look at yourself in the mirror and feel proud of who you are.

Nandini felt tears prick her eyes, but they were tears of happiness, of gratitude for having found this man who saw the world not as it was but as it could be. She leaned across the table and kissed him softly, tasting chocolate and promises on his lips.

That night, back in their room, they made love with the tender intensity of newlyweds who had chosen each other against all odds. The old bed creaked gently beneath them, a rhythmic accompaniment to their whispered endearments and quiet laughter. Moonlight filtered through the gauze curtains, casting silver patterns on their intertwined bodies as they moved together in the ancient dance of love and commitment.

Afterward, as they lay wrapped in each other's arms, Nandini traced lazy circles on Ajay's chest with her fingertip. "I love the way you make me feel," she whispered. "Like I'm exactly where I'm supposed to be."

"You are.....?," he murmured against her hair, breathing in the scent of jasmine from her shampoo. "We both are."

The next morning, they woke to the sound of temple bells echoing across the valley, a melodious call to prayer that seemed to bless their union. They stood on their balcony, wrapped in the quilt from their bed, watching the sun paint the sky in shades of gold and rose. The valley below was shrouded in mist, creating an otherworldly landscape that seemed to exist outside of time.

"It's like we're the only two people in the world," Nandini said softly, her head resting on Ajay's shoulder.

"Maybe we are," he replied, pressing a kiss to the top of her head. "Maybe this is our world, and everything else is just... background noise."

They spent the morning exploring the local market, where Ajay insisted on buying Nandini a shawl woven from the finest Kashmir wool. The vendor, an elderly woman with kind eyes and silver hair braided with colourful ribbons, smiled as she wrapped it around Nandini's shoulders.

"You have a good husband," she said in Hindi, her weathered hands adjusting the shawl with practiced care. "He looks at you like you're the most precious thing in the world."

Nandini blushed, her cheeks turning the colour of the hill station's famous strawberries. "He is good," she agreed in Hindi, her voice shy but proud.

As they walked away, Ajay slipped his arm around her waist, pulling her close. "What did she say?"

"That you look at me like I'm precious," Nandini replied, her eyes sparkling with mischief.

"You are precious," he said seriously. "More precious than all the corporate salaries and society's approval in the world."

After lunch at a quaint café overlooking the Arthur's Seat point, they decided to take a boat ride on the Venna Lake. The wooden boat, painted in bright blue and yellow, bobbed gently on the calm water as the boatman, a weather-beaten man with a ready smile, rowed them toward the centre of the lake.

"Sir, Madam, you want photo?" he asked, producing an old digital camera from somewhere in his boat. "Very good for memory."

They nodded, and he began clicking pictures of them in various poses—Ajay with his arm around Nandini, both of them laughing at something only they could hear; Nandini feeding ducks from a packet of bread crumbs they'd brought; Ajay trying to row while Nandini held onto his arms, both of them doubled over with laughter when he nearly dropped the oar.

As the sun began to set, painting the water in shades of amber and crimson, they found themselves in a quiet corner of the lake, surrounded by nothing but the gentle lapping of water against the boat and the distant call of evening birds.

"I want to remember this forever," Nandini said, her voice barely above a whisper.

"We will," Ajay promised, turning to face her in the small boat. "No matter what happens, we'll always have this. This moment, this feeling, this choice we made together. "He pulled her close, and they kissed as the sun dipped below the horizon, their silhouettes reflected in the still water like a promise written in liquid gold.

The Photoshoot

The next day, as they were walking through the main market area of Mahabaleshwar, they encountered a photographer with a small setup near the strawberry farms. He was a young man, perhaps in his late twenties, with an artistic eye and a warm smile that immediately put them at ease.

"Sir, Madam, you are very beautiful couple," he said in accented English, his camera hanging around his neck like a familiar friend. "I am Rahul, professional photographer. I make very nice pictures for honeymoon couples. You want to see my work?"

He showed them a portfolio of stunning black and white photographs—couples laughing in strawberry fields, embracing against the backdrop of misty mountains, dancing in the rain. The images were romantic, artistic, and captured something essential about love that went beyond mere documentation.

"These are beautiful," Nandini said, genuinely impressed. "But we're not really..."

"We're newlyweds," Ajay said quietly, his hand finding hers. "This is our honeymoon."

Rahul's eyes lit up. "Perfect! I have special package for newlyweds. We shoot at different locations—strawberry farm, old temple, sunset point. Very reasonable price, and you get all photos in one hour."

They looked at each other, and without needing to speak, they both nodded. Why not? This was their time, their celebration of choosing each other. They deserved to have these memories captured.

The first location was a sprawling strawberry farm where the owner, a jovial farmer named Patil kaka, welcomed them with fresh strawberries and cream. Rahul positioned them among the rows of green plants heavy with red berries, the rolling hills of Mahabaleshwar forming a perfect backdrop.

"Hold the strawberry up to her lips," Rahul instructed Ajay, "like you're feeding her. Yes, perfect! Now look at each other, not at camera. Feel the love, show the love."

Ajay held a plump strawberry near Nandini's lips, both of them laughing as she pretended to bite it. In that moment, with the late afternoon sun casting golden light across the farm and the sweet scent of strawberries in the air, they felt like they were the only two people in the world.

"Beautiful!" Rahul exclaimed, his camera clicking rapidly. "Now, sir, sit on the ground. Madam, sit beside him, lean against his shoulder. Like you're having picnic."

They settled into the pose, Nandini's head resting on Ajay's shoulder as he played with the end of her dupatta. The intimacy of the moment was real, unforced, captured in their natural gestures and the way they seemed to gravitate toward each other. "Now look at each other," Rahul said softly, his voice barely audible above the clicking of his camera. "Think about your wedding day. Think about the promises you made."

They turned toward each other, and for a moment, the photographer, the farm, the entire world faded away. They were back in that simple courthouse, holding hands and promising to love each other despite everything. The look that passed between them was so intimate, so filled with promise and hope, that Rahul lowered his camera for a moment.

"This is why I love photography," he said quietly. "Sometimes you capture not just a moment, but a feeling that will last forever."

The second location was an old temple nestled in a grove of ancient trees, its stone pillars weathered by centuries of monsoons and sunshine. The evening light filtered through the canopy, creating a cathedral of golden beams that seemed to bless their presence.

"This temple is very old," Rahul explained as he adjusted his camera settings. "Local people say couples who photograph here will have long, happy marriage."

He positioned them on the temple steps, Nandini's dupatta flowing gracefully around her as Ajay sat beside her, his hand resting on her knee. The pose was traditional, respectful, but their eyes held a modern understanding of equality and partnership.

"Now, madam, put your hand on his," Rahul instructed. "Like you're blessing each other."

As Nandini placed her hand over Ajay's, they both felt the weight of tradition and the promise of their future. They were starting something new, building on the foundation of ancient wisdom but creating their own path.

"Perfect," Rahul murmured, his camera capturing the moment when their fingers intertwined. "Now I want some candid shots. Just be natural, talk to each other, ignore the camera."

They began talking quietly, their voices mixing with the sound of temple bells and evening birds. Ajay told her about his dreams for the children he wanted to teach, about creating a school that would nurture not just minds but souls. Nandini shared her vision of using her corporate skills to eventually fund such initiatives, of being partners in both love and purpose.

As they talked, Rahul moved around them like a skilled dancer, his camera capturing unguarded moments—the way Ajay's eyes crinkled when he smiled, the graceful gesture of Nandini's hands as she spoke, the moment when they both laughed at the same memory.

The final location was Sunset Point, where the sky was already beginning to turn colours as the sun prepared for its daily farewell. Other couples and families were scattered around the viewpoint, but Rahul found them a quiet spot near the edge where the valley spread out below them like a green carpet. "This is the most romantic time," he said, checking his camera one more time. "Golden hour, we call it. Everything looks beautiful in this light."

He was right. The warm, golden light seemed to wrap around them like a blessing, softening every line and shadow. Nandini had changed into a flowing kurta the colour of sunset, and Ajay had rolled up his sleeves and unbuttoned his shirt collar, looking relaxed and happy.

"I want you to dance," Rahul said unexpectedly. "Like you did on wedding night. No music, just feel the rhythm in your hearts."

They looked at each other and laughed, suddenly shy again. But then Ajay extended his hand, and Nandini took it, and they began to sway together as they had in their little apartment. There was no music except the sound of the wind through the trees and the distant murmur of other visitors, but they moved together as if they could hear a symphony.

Rahul's camera captured it all—the way Ajay spun Nandini gently, her kurta floating around her like flower petals; the moment when she stumbled slightly and he caught her, both of them laughing; the instant when they stopped dancing and simply held each other, their foreheads touching, their eyes closed in perfect contentment.

"Last shot," Rahul said, his voice soft with emotion. "I want you to look at the sunset together. Think about your future. Think about all the sunsets you'll watch together."

They turned toward the setting sun, Ajay's arms around Nandini from behind, her hands resting on his arms. The sky was painted in shades of gold and pink and purple, the colours shifting and changing like a living canvas. In the distance, the valley stretched endlessly, green and peaceful and full of promise.

"This is just the beginning," Ajay whispered against her ear, his voice filled with wonder at the beauty of the moment and the certainty of their love.

"I know," Nandini replied, leaning back against his chest. "And I'm not afraid anymore. Whatever comes, we'll face it together."

As the sun dipped below the horizon, painting the sky in one final burst of colour, Rahul took the last photograph—two silhouettes against the infinite sky, holding each other as the world turned toward night.

An hour later, as promised, Rahul presented them with a collection of photographs that took their breath away. The images were more than just pictures; they were poetry captured in light and shadow, love made visible in glances and gestures and the way they moved together as if they were two parts of one whole.

"These are beautiful," Nandini said, her voice thick with emotion as she looked through the prints. "You've captured something... I don't know how to describe it."

"Love," Rahul said simply. "I've captured love. And love, when it's real like yours, is the most beautiful thing in the world."

They selected their favourites—the strawberry farm shot that showed them laughing together, the temple photograph that captured their sense of sacred commitment, and the sunset silhouette that spoke of endless possibilities. These images would travel with them through all the years that followed, reminders of this perfect weekend when they had chosen each other and been chosen by something larger than themselves.

That night, their last in Mahabaleshwar, they made love with a passion intensified by the knowledge that they were creating not just physical intimacy but emotional and spiritual connection. The photographs lay scattered on the small table by the window, catching the moonlight like fragments of dreams made real.

"I want to come back here," Nandini said as they lay entwined, her head on Ajay's chest, listening to the steady rhythm of his heartbeat.

"Every anniversary," Ajay promised, his fingers playing with her hair. "Every year, we'll come back and remember this moment, this choice, this love."

Building a Life Together

They settled into a modest and comfortable two-bedroom flat in a quiet neighbourhood where children played cricket in the narrow lanes and neighbours still greeted each other with genuine warmth. It wasn't luxurious by any stretch- the walls were freshly painted, the furniture was modest but nice, and the kitchen was barely large enough for two people- but it was theirs, filled with the warmth of shared dreams and mutual respect.

With Nandini's corporate job providing a steady income and occasional monetary support from their families—grudging but necessary—they were financially stable if not wealthy. Their fridge was always stocked with the basics and occasional treats, bills were paid on time without the anxiety that plagued so many young couples, and there was enough left over to eat out on weekends or buy storybooks for their someday child, building a small library that spoke of hope and planning for the future. They had found their rhythm, a comfortable dance of shared responsibilities and quiet contentment.

The photographs from Mahabaleshwar found their place of honour on the mantelpiece, arranged carefully between a small temple lamp and a vase that always held fresh marigolds. Every morning, as Ajay prepared for school and Nandini got ready for her corporate job, they would glance at those images and remember the weekend when they had chosen love over everything else. The photographs were more than memories; they were promises kept, dreams acknowledged, a visual reminder of what they were building together.

When their daughter, Pallavi, was born after a year of marriage, their world became brighter, infused with a joy so pure it seemed to illuminate every corner of their modest home. Ajay found new meaning in fatherhood, discovering reserves of tenderness he didn't know he possessed, and Nandini, despite juggling a hectic corporate job that demanded long hours and frequent travel, was a doting mother who somehow managed to make every moment with her daughter count. Pallavi was the glue that made every sacrifice feel worthwhile, every difficult choice validated by her innocent laughter and the way she reached for both parents with equal love and trust.

The Tragedy That Changed Everything

And then came the storm that would shatter everything they had built.

It was a Sunday afternoon, the kind of lazy day that families treasure, filled with the comfortable sounds of home and the promise of unhurried time together. The smell of cumin and onions wafted from the kitchen, mixing with the lingering aroma of the morning's tea, creating the familiar perfume of domestic contentment. Nandini was stirring dal on the stove, her movements automatic and soothing, while Pallavi, now in first standard and full of the confidence that comes with learning to read, was playing with crayons at the small dining table, her tongue poking out in concentration as she created another masterpiece.

The small apartment echoed with ordinary domestic sounds—the familiar whistle of the pressure cooker, the occasional hum of the television in the background, the comfortable silence of a family at ease with each other. In a moment of distraction, perhaps distracted by the cooking or simply assuming their six-year-old was safely occupied, Pallavi had climbed onto the gallery railing to get a better view of something that had caught her attention in the courtyard below. With the curiosity that defines childhood and the fearlessness that comes with innocence, she had pulled herself up on the metal bars, balancing precariously as she tried to see over the edge. And then: There was a sickening sound of impact against the concrete courtyard below, and then screams—whether from Pallavi or from the witnesses, Ajay would never know and would spend years trying to forget.

Ajay came running, his heart already knowing what his mind refused to accept, his feet carrying him faster than he had ever moved in his life. The neighbours gathered in a crowd that parted like the sea as he pushed through, their faces reflecting the horror he was about to confront. Time blurred into chaos—someone calling for an ambulance, someone else trying to direct traffic, voices raised in panic and confusion, hands reaching to help or hold back or simply to touch another human being in the face of tragedy.

The hospital, with its sterile corridors and fluorescent lights, declared her brought dead, the words falling like stones into the silence that followed. The colour drained from Nandini's face as if life itself was leaving her body, her skin taking on the grey pallor of shock that no amount of warmth could touch. She collapsed on the cold hospital bench, her body trembling with a grief that no words could console, no comfort could reach, no time could heal.

Nandini collapsed in grief that seemed to consume her very soul, her wails echoing through the hospital corridors like the cry of a wounded animal. A wave of horrifying emotions washed over Ajay and Nandini.

Why hadn't he watched her? Why wasn't he there when their daughter needed protection? Why had he failed in the most fundamental duty of a father? Sarita, ever present like a shadow of judgment, appeared at the hospital with the speed of a vulture drawn to tragedy, amplifying the blame with the skill of someone who had been waiting for this moment of vindication. Her words were sharp as surgical instruments, her tone accusatory and merciless, her verdict absolute and devastating: "He failed you. He failed your daughter. I warned you this would happen."

Sarita Deshmukh's venomous words never stopped, flowing like poison through phone calls and visits that left Nandini drained and questioning. Every conversation, every interaction was laced with criticism so sharp it could cut, painting Ajay as a failure, an anchor dragging her daughter down into a life of mediocrity and missed opportunities.

At first, Nandini brushed it off with the confidence of a woman secure in her choices, knowing the man she had married, understanding his worth in ways that transcended social conventions. But over time, like water wearing away stone, the seeds of doubt took root in the fertile soil of daily frustrations her mother created with her piercing notes.

The whispers of society grew louder in her mind, drowning out the quiet voice of contentment that had once guided her decisions. She smiled less, the bright laughter that had first attracted Ajay becoming increasingly rare. She laughed less, questioned more, and slowly, imperceptibly, began to withdraw from the partnership that had once been their strength.

The photographs from Mahabaleshwar, once a source of joy and remembered love, began to mock them from the mantelpiece. The couple in those images seemed like strangers now, their optimism naive, their promises hollow. The strawberry farm photograph that had once made them smile now seemed to taunt them with its innocent hope. The temple image, which had once symbolized their sacred commitment, now felt like evidence of their failure. The sunset silhouette, which had once represented infinite possibility, now looked like two people disappearing into darkness.

Within weeks, the distance between them became a canyon so wide that no bridge could span it. Nandini filed for divorce with the efficiency of someone who had already died inside, the legal proceedings swift and business-like in their destruction of what had once been beautiful. It was swift, uncontested, final—the paper dissolution of a love that had promised to last forever.

Ajay didn't protest, his voice lost in the desert of his own grief and guilt. What could he say? How could he argue with a pain so pure it cut through logic and reason? The love of his life had turned her back, and the child who had brought them joy was now nothing but ashes in a brass urn that sat on his mantelpiece like a monument to failure.

After mere seven years of marriage everything was lost. His nights became colder, quieter, unbearable stretches of darkness where sleep brought no peace and waking brought no relief. He kept Pallavi's last drawing—a rainbow with a smiling sun that seemed to mock him with its innocent optimism—framed on his desk where he could see it every day, a reminder of what he had lost and what he had failed to protect.

The photographs from their honeymoon, once displayed with

pride on the mantelpiece, were carefully packed away in a box that found its way to the back of his closet. He couldn't bear to look at them, but he couldn't bring himself to destroy them either. They were evidence of a different time, a different version of themselves, a different possibility that had been crushed by tragedy and blame.

Sometimes, in the darkest hours of sleepless nights, he would take out the box and hold one of the photographs, remembering the man he had been when the world still held promise, when love seemed stronger than loss, when the future stretched endlessly ahead like a sunset that would never end.

Redemption and New Purpose

For the next several days, Ajay drowned himself in teaching with the desperation of a man trying to outrun his demons. He arrived early when the school was still quiet and the corridors empty, stayed late when the janitors were cleaning and the security guards were making their rounds, and volunteered for every school event, every committee, every activity that could fill the empty hours and distract his mind from its endless cycle of grief and guilt.

He kept his weekends busy tutoring children from slums, providing them with uniforms and books and even food, finding in their hunger and hope a purpose that his own life had lost. The six girls; whom he had picked from the alleys of hardship and given them wings to fly beyond their circumstances, now in their early twenties, were on the verge of stepping into professional life. He called them his "stars," and they shone for him with the brightness of a dozen suns. Ajay was spending valuable time shaping their careers. Ajay was a father figure for them though they called him 'Sir'.

He remembered each of their birthdays- assigned by him alone- with the devotion of a priest remembering saints' days, wrote personal notes for their report cards that spoke of potential and promise, and believed with the fervour of a true believer that their success would somehow redeem his own broken past.

Second Chance

And then, one winter morning, as he took a detour through the crowded market on his way to school, fate delivered him a second chance wrapped in the most heart-breaking package imaginable. There she was—a frail, barefoot three-year-old, curled up like a discarded doll near a tea stall, shivering in the cold morning air that cut through her thin, torn clothes.

Her dark eyes, too large for her small face, were hollow with a pain that no child should ever know, but she wasn't crying—a detail that broke his heart more than tears ever could. She didn't even look scared, just empty, numb, as if the world had already taught her that hope was a luxury she couldn't afford.

She had no name that anyone knew, no family who claimed her, no voice that had been heard speaking in weeks. She was nothing and no one, invisible to a world that had too many problems to notice one more lost child.

He brought her home without hesitation, his decision made in the instant their eyes met and held. He bathed her gently, his large hands careful and tender as he washed away the dirt and grime of the streets, fed her with the patience of someone who understood that trust must be earned one spoonful at a time. That night, as she slept curled against him like a kitten seeking warmth, her small body finally relaxed for the first time in who knew how long, he whispered into the darkness, "Pallavi." A name not given in memory of what was lost, but in rebirth of what could be found, not as a replacement for his daughter but as a continuation of the love that had survived even the worst tragedy.

The next day, he began the formal adoption process, navigating the labyrinthine bureaucracy of the Indian legal system with the determination of a man on a mission. It was not easy—the paperwork was endless, forests of forms that demanded details he didn't have about a child whose past was a mystery, and the questions were uncomfortable, probing, designed to ensure he was worthy of the responsibility he was undertaking.

Social workers visited his modest flat, their clipboards and sceptical expressions making him feel like a defendant in a trial where the verdict was far from certain. But Ajay persisted with the stubborn patience of someone who had already lost everything and refused to lose anything more. He would not let her slip away, would not allow the system to swallow her back into the anonymity from which he had rescued her.

He told no one about his plans, not his family, not his colleagues, not even his closest friends. He didn't want sympathy or advice or well-meaning interference. He just wanted to rebuild what life had shattered, to create from the ashes of his loss something beautiful and lasting.

By the time she turned four, Pallavi was enrolled in Jr. KG at Vidya Vihar, the same school where Ajay had now completed ten years of dedicated service. He taught Standard 1 in the main building and often found excuses to visit the junior wing to check on her, his heart swelling with pride every time he saw her small hand raised in class or heard her voice joining in the morning songs.

Their bond was quiet, instinctive, built not on blood but on something deeper—the recognition of two souls who had found each other in the darkness. She called him "Daddy" without being taught, the word emerging naturally from her lips as if it had always been there, waiting.

He packed her lunchbox with cartoon-shaped parathas and notes that said "I love you" in his careful handwriting, small gestures that spoke of a devotion that had nothing to do with obligation and everything to do with choice. They walked to school holding hands—teacher and student, father and daughter, two people who had learned that family is not about genetics but about the decision to love and be loved.

In his desk drawer, hidden beneath stacks of lesson plans and student worksheets, Ajay kept a small box containing the photographs from Mahabaleshwar. Sometimes, when Pallavi was asleep and the night was particularly quiet, he would take them out and study them as if they were maps to a country he had once visited but could never return to.

The young man in those photographs looked familiar but distant, like a brother he had once known but had lost touch with over the years. The woman beside him in the images seemed like a character from a story he had read long ago, beautiful and real but existing in a different world, a different time, a different possibility.

But gradually, as his new Pallavi grew and thrived, as her laughter filled the empty spaces in his apartment and her trust rebuilt the broken places in his heart, those photographs began to take on a different meaning. They were no longer reminders of loss but proof of what was possible, evidence that love could exist, that two people could choose each other against all odds, that happiness was not a myth but a reality that could be touched, held, lived.

The man in those photographs had loved completely and been loved completely in return, and that experience, brief as it was, had changed him permanently, made him capable of the love he now gave to his adopted daughter.

Together, they rebuilt a life that was simple, quiet, and complete in ways that his previous existence, for all its promise and potential, had never been. The photographs from Mahabaleshwar, once painful reminders of what he had lost, became gentle teachers showing him what he had gained—the knowledge that love, in all its forms, was the only thing that truly mattered, the only thing that survived loss and time and the cruelty of fate.

But fate, as if unsatisfied with the happiness they had carved from sorrow, was preparing to test him once again.

Chapter 2: The Accusation

A touch Misunderstood

The morning sun filtered through the glass windows of Standard 1-B, casting long golden rectangles across the worn wooden floor. Dust motes danced in the light as if celebrating a new day, their tiny forms swirling in lazy spirals that seemed to mock the gravity of what was about to unfold. The classroom buzzed with the innocent energy of twenty-eight six-year-olds, their laughter mixing with the soft rustling of pages being turned and pencils scratching across paper.

At the front, Ajay Sharma stood with his sleeves rolled up to his elbows, chalk in hand, his voice soft but animated with the passion that made him beloved among his students.

"Children, when you look at the moon, do you think it's following you?" he asked, a familiar twinkle playing in his dark eyes as he gazed at the eager faces before him.

A chorus of giggles followed, the sound as pure and joyful as temple bells. One boy, his hair standing up in unruly spikes, shouted with the confidence that only comes from childhood, "Yes, sir! I thought it followed me on my cycle!"

Ajay laughed, his eyes lighting up with the genuine delight that had never dimmed despite all his personal losses. "That's because the moon wants to be your friend," he said, his voice carrying the warmth of someone who truly believed in the magic he was teaching.

These are the moments that make everything worthwhile, he thought, watching their faces transformed with wonder. This is why I became a teacher—to see this spark of discovery, this pure joy in learning.

Another child raised her hand eagerly, bouncing in her seat with excitement. "Sir, sir! Does the sun follow us too?"

"What do you think, Priya?" Ajay asked, moving closer to her desk with the fluid grace of someone who had perfected this dance over twelve years.

"I think... I think the sun is too busy keeping everyone warm!" she declared, her logic impeccable in its childish simplicity.

"Brilliant!" Ajay exclaimed, clapping his hands together. "The sun is indeed very busy, isn't it? Taking care of all the flowers, all the trees, all the children in the world."

Look at them, he mused, scanning the room as more hands shot up with theories about celestial behaviour. So eager, so trusting, so ready to believe in magic. This is what childhood should be—wonder, not worry.

It was these moments—unscripted, full of wonder, crackling with the electricity of young minds discovering the world—that made teaching worthwhile for him. He believed with every fibre of his being that childhood was not just a stage to be endured but a sacred space to be protected, and he guarded it fiercely against the harsh realities that waited beyond the classroom walls.

His gentle approach, storytelling style that turned every lesson into an adventure, and patient encouragement that never rushed or judged made him a beloved figure in the school corridors. He often walked among the students during lessons, his tall frame moving gracefully between the tiny desks, crouching beside them with the fluid motion of someone who had done this dance thousands of times, helping them form their letters and numbers, never rushing, always reassuring.

The Moment That Changed Everything

"Now, let's see how well you've been practicing your spelling," he said, his voice carrying the enthusiasm of someone who genuinely believed that each correctly spelled word was a small victory worth celebrating.

The children immediately bent over their notebooks, their little tongues poking out in concentration as they wrestled with the mysteries of written language. Ajay moved among them like a conductor orchestrating a symphony, pausing here to encourage, there to guide, everywhere to nurture.

Every child is different, he reminded himself, a mantra he'd developed over the years. Each one needs something slightly different from me. Some need confidence, some need challenge, some just need to know that someone believes in them.

He had a special way of noticing when a child was struggling—a sixth sense developed over twelve years of teaching that allowed him to spot the subtle signs of confusion or distress that other adults might miss. He lifted them—metaphorically, and sometimes literally—with the instinctive care of someone who understood that a child's confidence was as fragile as spun glass.

As he surveyed the room, his teacher's radar immediately picked up on something amiss. While the others were busy with their spelling practice, their tongues poking out in concentration, he noticed Nisha, a shy girl who rarely raised her hand and seemed to shrink into herself whenever attention turned her way. Her posture was slouched, her small shoulders curved inward as if she were trying to disappear, her pencil gripped too tightly in fingers that trembled slightly with anxiety.

Something's wrong, he noted, his heart immediately going out to her. She looks... defeated. No child should look defeated at six years old.

Her notebook revealed chaotic handwriting—letters tangled together like fallen branches, words misspelled with the creative inventiveness that comes from genuine effort meeting inadequate instruction. He walked to her desk with the quiet purpose of a doctor approaching a patient, and gently crouched beside her, his knees creaking slightly as he brought himself down to her level.

She's been struggling all week, he thought, remembering her previous assignments. Her mother mentioned she gets anxious about school work. I need to be extra gentle here.

"Nisha, would you come up here for a moment?" he asked kindly, his voice pitched low so as not to embarrass her in front of her classmates.

She looked up, startled, her large eyes widening with the fear that always seemed to live just beneath the surface of her expression. For a moment, she didn't move, as if hoping she might become invisible if she stayed perfectly still.

"It's okay, beta," Ajay said softly, using the endearment that came naturally to him with all his students. "I just want to help you with your spelling. Nothing to worry about."

She obeyed with the automatic compliance of a child who had learned that resistance only made things worse, her small feet shuffling across the floor as if she were walking to her execution.

Standing at the board with her tiny fingers clutching the corner of her notebook like a lifeline, she looked anxious, her small body radiating the tension of someone who expected criticism or disappointment. The other children had paused in their work, sensing the shift in classroom dynamics with the intuitive awareness that children possess.

Ajay pointed to a drawing of an elephant that he had sketched earlier, "Nisha, see this? You wrote 'elefunt.' What do we call this animal?" he asked, his voice carrying none of the impatience that might have crept into another teacher's tone.

Don't let her feel embarrassed, he coached himself. Make this about learning, not about being wrong.

"Elephant," she whispered, barely audible, her voice so soft it was almost swallowed by the ambient noise of the classroom.

"That's right. Perfect!" Ajay said with genuine enthusiasm. "And how do we spell it?" he asked with the same warmth, hoping to ease her nervousness with his steady presence and encouraging smile.

She hesitated again, her mouth opening and closing like a fish out of water, the correct spelling dancing just beyond her grasp. Her eyes darted around the room, as if the answer might be written on the walls.

She knows this, Ajay thought. She's just too nervous to remember. I need to help her relax.

Ajay bent slightly, bringing himself to her level with the natural grace of someone who had spent years communicating with children. Without a second thought, driven by the same instinct that had made him a beloved teacher for over a decade, he ran a comforting hand over her head, his palm gentle against her soft hair, the way a parent might reassure a child or a teacher might encourage a struggling student.

"It's okay. We'll learn together," he said gently, his voice carrying the promise of patience and understanding that had made him a sanctuary for countless children over the years.

This is what teaching is about, he thought, his hand resting briefly on her head in the universal gesture of comfort and encouragement. Letting them know they're not alone, that making mistakes is part of learning.

But something strange happened. Nisha's lips quivered as if touched by an invisible wind. Her eyes brimmed with tears that seemed to come from nowhere, confusion and fear mixing in their depths. Though she wasn't hurt—not physically, not in any way that an adult observer could identify—something had shifted inside her fragile psyche.

"I... I don't know," she whispered, her voice trembling with an emotion that seemed disproportionate to the simple spelling exercise.

Ajay felt a flicker of concern. What's wrong? This is such a small thing. Why does she look so frightened?

"It's perfectly fine, Nisha," he said, his voice even gentler. "E-L-E-P-H-A-N-T. See? Now you know. Would you like to try writing it again?"

She nodded quickly, too quickly, and returned to her seat with hurried steps, her head down, her shoulders hunched as if trying to shield herself from invisible threats.

Something's not right, Ajay thought, watching her retreat. That reaction was... unusual. I should talk to her mother next week during parent-teacher meetings.

The innocence of the gesture had collided with a world outside the classroom—a world her mother had described again and again in serious tones, painting scenarios of danger where none had existed before. At home, Nisha had been hearing about "good touch" and "bad touch" for weeks, the concepts delivered with the repetitive intensity of a safety drill. Ever since the media had exploded over a horrific abuse case in another school—headlines screaming of violated innocence and shattered trust—her mother had been vigilant to the point of paranoia, turning every bedtime into a safety briefing, every casual physical contact into a potential threat.

The rest of the class continued, but Ajay found himself stealing glances at Nisha, who sat hunched over her notebook, her pencil moving mechanically across the page. The other children seemed oblivious to the strange moment, their attention already captured by the next activity—a singing game about animals that usually had them giggling and clapping.

Maybe I'm overthinking this, he told himself. Children have emotional moments. She's always been sensitive. This is probably nothing.

But the nagging feeling persisted as he led the class through their morning routine, the strange encounter casting a shadow over what should have been a perfectly normal day.

Now, even love felt confusing to a six-year-old mind that was being asked to navigate complexities that adults struggled to understand.

The Seeds of Suspicion

That evening, Nisha returned home unusually quiet, her normal chatter replaced by a silence that seemed to echo through the small apartment. She didn't run to show her art or sing the new rhyme she'd learned, rituals that usually marked the transition from school to home. Instead, she simply slipped off her shoes with mechanical precision and sat on the floor, drawing circles on her notebook with the obsessive repetition of someone trying to make sense of something that defied understanding.

Her mother, Smita Kulkarni, noticed immediately with the hypervigilance of a parent who had been primed to see danger everywhere. The absence of her daughter's usual animated recounting of the day's events was as loud as a fire alarm.

"Nishu, how was school today?" she asked, setting down her office bag and crouching beside her daughter. "You're very quiet. Are you feeling alright?"

Nisha continued drawing her circles, each one darker than the last, her pencil pressing harder into the paper with each repetition.

"What happened at school, Nishu?" Smita asked again, her

voice carrying the edge of concern that mothers develop when their instincts are triggered.

Nisha looked away, her eyes focused on the patterns she was drawing, her voice barely above a whisper. "Sir picked me up and touched my head," she said in a trembling voice that carried the weight of confusion and fear. "I was crying because of my notebook."

Smita froze, her blood turning to ice in her veins as every warning she had heard, every horror story she had read, every parental nightmare she had imagined suddenly crystallized into this moment. The coffee mug in her hand seemed to weigh a thousand pounds.

No, she thought, her mind immediately jumping to the worst-case scenarios. Not my daughter. Not in her school. Not with a teacher we trusted.

"Did it feel wrong, sweetheart?" she asked, her voice carefully controlled despite the panic rising in her chest like flood water.

"I don't know, Mom... maybe it was bad. Or maybe good," Nisha mumbled, her child's honesty more terrifying than any accusation could have been. "He touched my hair and said we'll learn together."

'Maybe it was bad'—oh God, what does that mean? Smita's mind raced. She doesn't even know. She's confused. This is exactly what all the articles said—children don't always understand what's happening to them.

Smita's face hardened as her maternal instincts warred with her rational mind. The blurred line between affection and suspicion had never felt more dangerous, more impossible to navigate. She didn't want to overreact, didn't want to destroy an innocent man's life based on a child's confused recollection, but she couldn't ignore it either, couldn't risk her daughter's safety for the sake of politeness or giving someone the benefit of the doubt.

"Nishu, listen to me carefully," she said, taking her daughter's hands in hers. "You did nothing wrong, okay? Nothing at all. You're a good girl, and Mom is proud of you for telling me."

I need to call Raghav. I need to think clearly. I need to protect my daughter, but I also need to be fair. God, what if I'm wrong? What if I'm right? What if the story of the stranger is true?

She waited for her husband, Raghav, to return home, the minutes stretching like hours as she watched her daughter's every gesture for signs of trauma or distress. She made dinner mechanically, her mind spinning with possibilities and fears, each scenario worse than the last.

What if this has been going on for weeks? What if she's been too scared to tell me? What if there are other children?

When Raghav finally arrived, his engineering mind immediately shifting into analysis mode as he saw his wife's expression, she pulled him into their bedroom and closed the door.

"Something happened at school," she began, her voice tight with controlled emotion. "With Nisha's teacher."

Over dinner, with Nisha safely in bed after being unusually compliant about bedtime, she recounted the incident with the clinical precision of someone delivering evidence in a court case.

"She was confused, Raghav. Scared, even. You know what happened last month at that international school—the headlines, the investigations, the children who will never be the same. We can't take chances with our daughter's safety."

Raghav listened carefully, his mind trying to process the implications and possibilities. "But touching her head... that could be innocent, couldn't it? Teachers do that all the time."

"But what if it wasn't?" Smita countered, her voice rising

slightly. "What if that's just what she's willing to tell us? What if there's more that she's too scared or too confused to say?"

"A week ago, I met a person whose granddaughter studied in the same school. He had a bad experience with Ajay Sir. He specifically told me to teach my daughter about good touch and bad touch. I never thought that my daughter would also………". Smita teared up."

She's right, Raghav thought reluctantly. In today's world, we can't afford to give anyone the benefit of the doubt when it comes to our children.

"Let's go to the school. Talk to the principal. We won't accuse anyone—we'll just explain our concern and let them handle it properly."

"And if they don't take it seriously?" Smita asked, her voice carrying the steel of a mother prepared to fight for her child.

"Then we'll take it higher. Police, education department, media if necessary. But let's start with the school. Give them a chance to do the right thing."

Neither of them slept well that night, both lying awake wondering if they were overreacting or if they weren't reacting strongly enough.

Principal's Dilemma

Principal Ms. Vandana Joshi sat upright in her wooden chair, her hands clasped tightly on the polished table that had witnessed countless difficult conversations over her twenty-year career, when Smita and Raghav arrived. They were visibly uneasy—less confrontational than many parents she had dealt with, more torn between concern and doubt, their faces reflecting the internal struggle of people who wanted to do the right thing but weren't sure what that meant.

Here we go again, she thought with weary resignation. Another accusation, another teacher's life in the balance, another family torn apart by suspicion and fear.

"Thank you for seeing us on such short notice," Raghav began, clearing his throat nervously. "Madam, we've come with a serious concern. Yesterday, our daughter Nisha came home disturbed. She said her teacher, Mr. Ajay Sharma, picked her up and touched her."

Ms. Joshi felt the familiar chill that ran down her spine whenever such accusations arose, even as she maintained her professional composure. “Please explain exactly what she told you.” she said, her voice professional but not unkind.

Not Ajay, she thought desperately. Anyone but Ajay. He's the best teacher we have, the most dedicated, the most caring. This can't be happening.

Smita repeated Nisha's words, softening none of the details, her voice steady despite the turmoil in her heart, and adding, "She wasn't sure if it was bad or good, but she was afraid. We've been educating her about personal safety ever since that incident in the other school. It's difficult to tell what's harmless anymore in times like these."

Ms. Joshi nodded; her expression carefully neutral despite the storm of conflicting emotions in her chest. "I understand your concern completely. Mr. Sharma is one of our senior-most and most respected teachers—twelve years without a single complaint, beloved by students and parents alike. But we will take this seriously. We have to, given the climate we're operating in."

How do I handle this? she wondered. How do I protect the school, protect Ajay, protect this child, all at the same time? How do I navigate this minefield without destroying innocent lives?

Raghav leaned forward, his voice earnest. "Madam, we're not here to defame the school or destroy anyone's reputation. But if this matter is ignored, and something more serious happens later, can you imagine the consequences? The media attention, the legal ramifications, the damage to innocent children?"

"There will be no ignoring," Ms. Joshi assured them, though her heart was breaking for Ajay even as she spoke. "We have protocols for these situations. I will speak with Mr. Sharma immediately, and we will conduct a thorough investigation. Please, give me some time to look into this properly. I request you, for now, not to discuss it with other parents. Let us handle this with discretion and ensure that everyone's rights are protected."

I have to protect the school, she reasoned. But I also have to protect Ajay. Maybe this is just a misunderstanding. Maybe I can resolve this quietly without destroying his career.

The couple agreed, though unease lingered in their eyes like storm clouds that promised more turbulence ahead. As they left, Ms. Joshi sat back in her chair, her face drawn with the conflict of someone who had to balance institutional protection with personal loyalty.

What am I supposed to do? she asked herself. Call the board? Call the police? Suspend Ajay pending investigation? Every option feels like a betrayal of someone.

She trusted Ajay—but the times were unforgiving, and innocent intentions meant nothing in the court of public opinion. Her phone buzzed with a text from the board chairman: "Any issues I should know about?" The timing felt ominous, as if the very walls had ears.

I have to call him in. I have to hear his side. And then... God help me, I have to decide whether to destroy a good man's life to protect this institution.

The Confrontation

Ajay entered the principal's office later that afternoon, his footsteps echoing in the corridors that were quieter now, most of the children having gone home to their families and afternoon snacks. He had just finished music class and still carried a tambourine in his hand, the instrument somehow looking foolish and innocent in the gravity of the moment. He placed it on a chair and adjusted his sleeves, a nervous habit he had developed over the years.

"Good afternoon, ma'am," he said cheerfully, still unaware of the storm that was about to break over his head. "You wanted to see me?"

"Please sit, Ajay," Ms. Joshi said, her voice carrying a weight that made him immediately alert.

Something's wrong, he thought, his teacher's instincts kicking in. She looks like she's about to deliver bad news. Have I done something wrong? Is there a problem with one of my students?

He sensed something was wrong with the instinct of someone who had learned to read the subtle signs of distress in others. Her voice was heavier than usual, her posture more rigid, her eyes avoiding his with the deliberate care of someone avoiding a painful sight.

"Is everything alright, ma'am? You seem... troubled."

"I received a complaint today from the parents of Nisha Kulkarni," she began, the words falling like stones into the silence between them. "They claim you touched their daughter inappropriately."

The word hit him like a physical blow. For a moment, he couldn't breathe, couldn't think, couldn't process what he was hearing. What? What did she just say? Inappropriately? Nisha? ....Impossible! Something is wrong.

Ajay blinked, the word "inappropriately" echoing in his mind like a curse. "Touched? I… I only ran my hand over her head. She was crying, struggling with her spelling. It was instinct. A teacher's instinct—the same gesture I've made thousands of times with hundreds of children."

This can't be happening, he thought, his mind reeling. This is insane. I was helping her. I was being kind. How can kindness be twisted into something so horrible?

Ms. Joshi leaned back, her chair creaking under the weight of the moment. "The parents interpreted it differently. Given the sensitivity around child safety, especially after the recent incident that's been all over the news, we can't overlook it, no matter how innocent the intention might have been."

"But you know me!" Ajay said, his voice rising with desperation. "You know I would never... I could never... Children are everything to me. They're the reason I became a teacher!"

This is a nightmare, he thought. This has to be a nightmare. I'll wake up and this will all be gone.

Ajay's voice trembled with the desperation of someone watching his world crumble. "You know me, ma'am. I've been here twelve years. Not a single complaint. Not a blemish on my record. I've given my life to this school, to these children. I've missed my own family functions, my own health, my own happiness for these children."

"I believe you, Ajay. Personally, completely, without reservation. But this has gone beyond belief, beyond personal trust. The management is under pressure from the board, from parents, from the media climate we're operating in. The safe route is to ask for your resignation—quiet, dignified, without any formal proceedings."

Resignation? The word hit him like a slap. My career, my

reputation, my life's work—all gone because I comforted a crying child?

"You're asking me to quit?" he whispered, his voice hoarse with disbelief. "You're asking me to destroy my own reputation, to admit guilt for something I didn't do?"

"I'm trying to protect you, Ajay. If this becomes public, if there's an investigation, if the media gets hold of it... your life will be over regardless of the outcome."

Ajay stood, his chest rising and falling with the rapid breathing of someone in crisis. "No. I won't resign. Because I'm not guilty of anything except caring about a child who was struggling. If I resign, everyone will assume I'm guilty. My daughter will grow up thinking her father was a predator."

Pallavi, he thought with a stab of pain. What will this do to her? She's already lost so much. She can't lose her faith in me too.

Ms. Joshi sighed; her eyes dim with the sadness of someone forced to betray a friend. "Then the school will be compelled to take official action. The board will demand it. The parents will demand it. I didn't want it to come to this, but my hands are tied."

"What kind of official action?" Ajay asked, though he dreaded the answer. "A formal complaint. Police investigation. Suspension pending inquiry. Media attention. All the things I was hoping to spare you."

My God, Ajay thought, the full horror of his situation finally sinking in. This is really happening. This is my life now. Suspicion, investigation, disgrace—all because I touched a child's head.

"I need time to think," he said quietly. "Can you give me that much?"

"Twenty-four hours, Ajay. That's all I can give you. After that, I have to report this to the board, and they'll make the decision for both of us."

The Unofficial Call

That evening, Ms. Joshi stood by her desk as the last light of day faded from the windows. The school bell had rung hours ago, but she hadn't left, couldn't bring herself to go home to her own family while this situation remained unresolved.

I have to do something, she thought, pacing back and forth in her office. I can't let this drag on. I can't let the school be destroyed by scandal, but I also can't let Ajay be destroyed by false accusations.

She stared at her phone for a long time, her finger hovering over the contact for Sub-Inspector Patil, a man she had dealt with before on school matters—mostly minor incidents, nothing like this.

Maybe if I call him unofficially, he can handle this quietly. Maybe he can scare Ajay into resigning, or maybe he can convince the parents that this is much ado about nothing.

With trembling fingers that betrayed her professional composure, she dialled Sub-Inspector Patil's personal number.

"Patil Sir, it's Vandana Joshi from Vidya Vihar School. I hope I'm not disturbing you."

"Not at all, madam. What can I do for you?"

"There's a situation here at the school," she began, her voice carefully controlled. "One of our teachers is being accused of misconduct. We need your help to handle this delicately."

There was a pause on the other end. "What kind of misconduct, madam?"

"A parent says he touched their daughter inappropriately. I know the teacher—he's been with us for twelve years, never had any issues. But given the current climate..."

"Should we file a case, madam?"

"No. Not yet. Can you just... pay him a visit? Off the record, nothing official. Give him a scare, make him understand the gravity of the situation. Maybe get his resignation voluntarily. We'd like to avoid public attention, media scrutiny, anything that might damage the school's reputation or traumatize the children further."

I'm doing this for everyone's good, she told herself. For the school, for the children, even for Ajay. This is the kindest way to handle it.

"Understood, madam," Patil said, his tone suggesting he had handled similar situations before. "We'll handle it discreetly, professionally. Sometimes a conversation is all that's needed to resolve these misunderstandings."

"Thank you, Patil Sir. I appreciate your help."

She hung up and closed her eyes, the weight of her decision settling on her shoulders like a physical burden. The walls of her office had never felt so heavy, so confining, so complicit in the destruction of a good man's life.

I had no choice, she whispered to the empty room. I had no choice.

The Inquiry

Ajay sat on his sofa, staring at the wall, his mind churning with the events of the day. He had barely eaten dinner, barely spoken to Pallavi, barely acknowledged her cheerful chatter about her day at the neighbour's house.

How do I explain this to her? he wondered. How do I tell a six-year-old that her father is being accused of something horrible? How do I maintain her innocence while my world falls apart?

He was helping Pallavi arrange her toy animals on the small

dining table, the simple domestic ritual providing a momentary distraction from the day's trauma, when there was a knock at the door. Sharp, authoritative, unlike the gentle tapping of neighbours or the familiar rhythm of the grocery boy.

Who could that be at this hour? he thought, glancing at the clock. It's almost eight o'clock.

He assumed it was the grocery boy running late, but instead, two plainclothes officers stood outside, their presence filling the doorway with an ominous authority that made his mouth go dry.

Oh God, he thought, his heart sinking. They're here. It's really happening.

"Mr. Ajay Sharma?" The older officer's voice was neutral, professional, giving nothing away.

"Yes." The word came out as barely a whisper.

"We're from the Shivajinagar police station. We'd like you to come with us. A few routine questions, nothing more."

Routine questions? About what? About the accusation? About my life? About my reputation?

Ajay frowned, his mind racing through possibilities. "I haven't been served any notice. What's this about? What routine questions?"

"We can explain at the station. Don't worry—it's just a conversation, nothing formal," one officer said, his tone suggesting this was not really a request.

Just a conversation, Ajay thought bitterly. Just a conversation that will destroy my life, my career, my daughter's future.

Pallavi clung to Ajay's shirt, her small fingers grasping the fabric with the desperation of someone who sensed danger even if she couldn't name it. "Daddy, don't go..." she whispered, her voice frightened, shaky.

Ajay's heart sank as her words— frightened, shaky, carrying the echo of every abandonment she had ever experienced—pierced through every layer of his composure. This child had already lost so much, had already been failed by the adults who should have protected her.

I can't leave her, he thought desperately. Not like this. Not when she's scared. Not when she needs me most.

He turned to the officers, his voice steady despite the chaos in his mind. "Please. I have a daughter at home. There's no one else to care for her. Give me a moment to make some arrangement for her, and then I'll come with you willingly."

The officers exchanged glances, and Ajay could see them weighing their options. They had expected a simple pickup, not a complicated domestic situation.

"I'm not going anywhere," Ajay said, his voice gaining strength. "I'm not running. I just need to make sure my daughter is safe."

The younger officer glanced at the girl, his expression softening slightly at the sight of her tear-filled eyes. "We'll wait five minutes. No more."

Five minutes to arrange my daughter's care. Five minutes to hold onto my dignity. Five minutes before my life changes forever.

The Call for Help

Ajay stepped inside, his hands trembling as he stared at the phone. The contact list on his phone seemed to mock him—so few numbers, so few people he could trust with his most precious responsibility.

Who can I call? Ms. Desai next door? She's too old to handle Pallavi alone. The neighbour downstairs? I barely know them. My brother? He's in Mumbai. My sister? She's in Bangalore.

He scrolled through his contacts, his finger hovering over name after name, each one representing a relationship that wasn't close enough, wasn't strong enough, wasn't dependable enough for this moment.

There's no one, he realized with growing panic. In all my years of building a life, I've built it around work and Pallavi. I have no support system. No close friends. No family nearby.

And then he saw it. A name he had never deleted, despite four years of silence. A number he had memorized but never dialled.

Nandini.

He wiped his face with the back of his hand, took a deep breath that felt like swallowing glass, and pressed the number he had never thought he would dial again.

"Nandini… it's Ajay. Please don't cut the call. I need you." His voice broke on the last word, four years of separation collapsing into this moment of desperate need.

There was silence on the other end, but he could hear her breath, could almost feel her shock and confusion traveling through the connection.

She's going to hang up, he thought. She's going to hang up and I'll have no one.

"Ajay?" Her voice was tentative, disbelieving. "Is this really you?"

"I… I've been accused of something terrible. There's no one here with Pallavi. Please. Just come. I'll explain everything when I can."

“Pallavi?” Another pause, longer this time. "Accused of what? What's happened?"

"I can't explain now. The police are here. They're waiting.

Please, Nandini. I know I have no right to ask, but... there's no one else."

I'm begging my ex-wife to save me, he thought with bitter irony. The woman I hurt, the woman I disappointed, the woman I drove away—she's my only hope.

"I'll be there in ten minutes," she said, her voice steady despite the obvious shock. "Don't worry about Pallavi. Just... be careful, Ajay."

The line went dead, and Ajay stared at the phone in his hand, amazed that she had agreed, terrified about what was coming next.

Ten minutes, he thought. I have to convince the police to wait ten minutes.

He walked back to the door, where the officers stood impatiently.

"My daughter's mother is coming," he said. "Ten minutes. Please."

"We said five minutes," the older officer replied.

"She's six years old," Ajay said, his voice carrying the weight of a father's desperation. "She's already lost her mother once. Please don't make her watch her father being taken away by police. Ten minutes. I'm not going anywhere."

The officers looked at each other, then at the small girl peering around the door frame, her eyes wide with fear and confusion.

"Fine. Ten minutes. But if you're not ready then, we'll have to proceed differently."

"Pallavi, beta, do you remember when I told you about your mama in heaven?"

She nodded, her eyes never leaving his face.

"Well, I had another friend, a long time ago, before you came to live with me. Her name is Nandini Auntie, and she's coming to stay with you for a little while."

"Where are you going, Daddy?" she asked, her voice small and frightened.

How do I explain this? How do I tell her that the world has gone mad, that kindness is being mistaken for cruelty, that her father is being branded a monster?

"I have to go talk to some people about work. It might take a while. But Nandini Auntie will take care of you, okay? She's... she's very special."

Pallavi's eyes filled with tears. "I don't want you to go."

"I don't want to go either, beta. But sometimes grown-ups have to do things they don't want to do. The important thing is that you're safe and loved."

Ten minutes felt like ten hours, but finally, the doorbell rang again.

The Reunion

Nandini stood in the doorway, framed by the light from the hallway, her face unreadable—a mixture of shock, concern, and something that might have been the ghost of old affection. She looked older, more tired, but her eyes still held the intelligence and strength that had first attracted him all those years ago.

She came, he thought, hardly able to believe it. After everything, she came.

Her eyes dropped to the little girl behind Ajay, clinging to his leg with the fierce possessiveness of someone who had already lost too much.

"This is Pallavi?" she whispered, her voice carrying a complex mix of emotions—surprise, recognition, and something that might have been maternal instinct awakening.

Ajay nodded; his eyes glassy with unshed tears. "Please stay with her. I'll explain everything when I return—if I return."

If I return, he thought, the words echoing in his mind like a death sentence. What if I don't? What if this is the last time, I see her?

Nandini stepped inside slowly, her movements careful and deliberate, her gaze still fixed on the child who bore the name of their lost daughter. She knelt down to Pallavi's level, her voice gentle.

"Hello, Pallavi. I'm Nandini. Your Daddy has told me so much about you."

Pallavi looked between her father and this strange woman, her child's intuition picking up on the undercurrents of emotion in the room.

"Are you going to take care of me?" she asked, her voice barely above a whisper.

"Yes, beta. I'm going to take very good care of you."

Ajay kissed the top of Pallavi's head, breathing in the sweet scent of her hair, memorising the tenderness of this embrace.

This might be the last time, he thought, his heart breaking. This might be the last time I hold her like this.

"I love you, Pallavi. Remember that, no matter what happens, no matter what anyone says. Your Daddy loves you more than anything in the world."

The door closed behind him with a soft click that sounded like the sealing of a tomb, leaving behind the two most important women in his life—one who had given him his greatest joy, and one who had given him his greatest sorrow.

As he walked toward the waiting police car, Ajay couldn't help but think about the cruel irony of it all. He had spent his entire adult life trying to heal from the loss of his first daughter, and now, in trying to help another child, he might lose the second daughter who had become his whole world.

God, he prayed silently as he got into the car, if you're listening, please don't let this destroy her too. She's already lost too much. Please don't let her lose faith in me.

The car pulled away from the curb, carrying him toward an uncertain future, while in his apartment, two strangers bonded by their love for him began the delicate process of learning to trust each other in the shadow of an unimaginable crisis.

Chapter 3: Shadows of the Past

From Teacher to Suspect

The police jeep crawled through the dim lanes of Shivajinagar like a predator stalking its prey, headlights casting uneasy shadows on walls lined with faded political posters and peeling paint that told stories of monsoons past. The streets were quieter than usual for a weeknight, a light fog curling along the roadside like a ghost refusing to leave its earthly domain. The mist seemed to swallow the amber glow of the streetlights, creating an otherworldly atmosphere that made the familiar neighbourhood feel alien and threatening.

Inside the cramped vehicle, Ajay sat between two constables, their khaki uniforms smelling of sweat and stale cigarettes. He stared ahead in silence, his reflection ghostlike in the windshield. The younger constable kept glancing at him with poorly concealed curiosity, while the older one maintained a studied indifference that spoke of years spent ferrying broken souls through the city's arteries of justice.

Ajay wasn't handcuffed—not yet—but the humiliation clawed at his spine like invisible chains, each link forged from the whispered accusations and suspicious glances that had followed him from the school. The shrill echo of the siren wasn't there—but in his mind, alarms rang louder than ever, drowning out the steady hum of the engine and the distant sounds of the city settling into an uneasy sleep.

His hands, those same hands that had guided hundreds of students through the maze of knowledge, now trembled slightly as they rested on his knees. These were the hands that had wiped away countless tears, that had applauded achievements both small and monumental, that had gently corrected homework and smoothed ruffled hair. Now they felt foreign to him, as if they belonged to someone else entirely—someone capable of the unthinkable.

Each pothole the vehicle hit sent a tremor through his bones, not because of the physical jolt, but because of what lay ahead. This was a world he'd never imagined stepping into—not even in his darkest nightmares. Not as a teacher who had dedicated his life to nurturing young minds, not as a father who had sacrificed everything for his adopted daughter, and certainly not as a man whose entire existence had been built on the quiet dignity of doing what's right.

The irony wasn't lost on him—like a knife twisting in an already bleeding wound. He who had dedicated his life to protecting children, who had made their welfare his sacred mission, was now accused of harming one. The thought made his stomach churn with a mixture of rage and helplessness. How had compassion become criminalized? When had a gentle touch become grounds for suspicion?

The streetlights flickered intermittently, casting dancing shadows across his weathered face. In the play of light and darkness, he saw fragments of his life—moments of joy with Pallavi, quiet evenings spent helping her with homework, the pride in her eyes when she mastered a difficult concept. Each memory felt precious now, fragile as spun glass, threatened by the ugly reality of his current situation.

He thought of Pallavi, probably fast asleep by now in her small bed, surrounded by her collection of stuffed animals and children's books. She would be unaware that her father's world was crumbling beneath his feet, that the man she trusted completely was being painted as a monster by people who had never bothered to truly know him. The innocence of her sleep felt like a rebuke to the cruelty of the adult world.

Would she understand when she woke up? Would she ask why

Papa hadn't come home to read her the bedtime story he'd promised? The questions multiplied in his mind like a plague of locusts, each one more painful than the last. He had always been her protector, her safe harbour in a world that had already shown her too much cruelty for her young years. Now, how could he protect her from the storm that was about to engulf them both?

The Police Station

The jeep turned abruptly, tires screeching against the asphalt, and stopped in front of the police station—a crumbling building that seemed to slouch under the weight of human misery. The structure bore the scars of bureaucratic neglect: rusted nameplates that had long since faded to illegibility, windows with iron bars that cast prison-like shadows, and walls that seemed to exhale the accumulated despair of countless souls who had passed through its doors.

The smell hit him as soon as he stepped out—a toxic cocktail of fatigue, fear, and institutional indifference that had been baked into the very walls over decades. It was the smell of dreams deferred, of justice delayed, of lives hanging in the balance while wheels of bureaucracy ground slowly forward.

Sub-Inspector Patil was already waiting, his bulky frame silhouetted against the harsh neon lights of the station entrance. A man in his late forties, Patil had the weathered look of someone who had seen too much of humanity's darker side. His face was hard, etched with lines that spoke of difficult decisions and moral compromises, but his eyes—when caught in the right light—still held a flicker of the idealism that had once driven him to join the force.

He had witnessed enough broken men and manipulative ones to distinguish between guilt and confusion, between the desperate lies of the cornered and the bewildered protests of the innocent. But tonight, he wasn't there to assess innocence or guilt. He was acting on the school principal's urgent request, following the unwritten rules of damage control that governed institutions more than justice. Procedure was secondary. Optics were everything.

"Mr. Sharma," Patil said, his voice carrying the weight of official authority but lacking the harsh edge of accusation. "Please come inside. We need to have a conversation."

Ajay nodded; his throat too dry to speak. As they walked through the entrance, he caught sight of the station's motto painted on the wall: "Satyameva Jayate" - Truth Alone Triumphs. The irony was bitter on his tongue.

The waiting area was a study in human suffering. It smelled of damp files that had absorbed years of moisture and despair, stale tea that had been brewing too long, and the sharp tang of anxiety that seemed to seep from the very pores of those who waited. An old fan creaked above them, its blades cutting through the thick air with the persistence of a metronome counting down to someone's doom.

A clerk sat behind a counter that had seen better decades, scribbling lazily in a register with the mechanical precision of someone who had long since stopped caring about the individual stories behind each entry. The wall clock ticked louder than it should have, its sound echoing off the concrete walls like a countdown to judgment.

This was the underbelly of society, where dreams came to die and reputations were buried alive without ceremony. It was a place where the powerful rarely ventured and the powerless came to learn that justice was a luxury they could not afford. Ajay had never imagined he would be sitting among them.

The realization hit him like a physical blow. This was his world now—not the classroom with its neat rows of desks and eager faces, not the staff room with its gentle camaraderie and shared purpose.

This was where his story would be written, in the harsh fluorescent light of institutional indifference, among the forgotten and the accused.

The Interrogation

Patil glanced at Ajay over his reading glasses, which perched precariously on his nose like a judgment waiting to fall. His expression was unreadable, neither hostile nor sympathetic. "So, you're the teacher," he said, his voice carrying the weight of inevitability.

Ajay cleared his throat, surprised by how small his voice sounded in the echoing chamber. "Yes. Ajay Sharma. May I know what the complaint is exactly? I've been told nothing beyond vague accusations."

The question hung in the air like a challenge. Around them, the sounds of the station continued—the scratch of pen on paper, the distant ringing of phones, the muffled conversations of constables discussing their shift rotations. But in their small corner of this bureaucratic purgatory, silence stretched between the two men like a chasm.

Patil set his pen down with a loud click that seemed to reverberate through the room. The sound was final, decisive, like a gavel falling. "Informal inquiry, Mr. Sharma. No FIR yet. But parents have alleged inappropriate conduct with a child. A very serious allegation. What do you have to say?"

The words hit Ajay like a physical assault. Inappropriate conduct. The clinical language made his skin crawl. It reduced a moment of human compassion to something sordid, something that needed to be investigated and catalogued and filed away in the growing mountain of society's failures.

His mouth went dry, tongue sticking to the roof of his mouth as if his own body was conspiring against him. "I'm innocent," he said, the words coming out as barely more than a whisper. He cleared his throat and tried again, with more force. "I comforted a crying student. That's all. She was upset about her homework, about her performance in class. I did what any teacher would do—what any human being should do."

The explanation sounded weak even to his own ears. How could he make them understand the complexity of that moment? How could he convey the child's vulnerability, her need for reassurance, the innocent trust in her eyes? Words seemed inadequate to capture the purity of intention that had driven his actions.

Patil scratched his stubble, a rasping sound that spoke of weariness and the late hour. His eyes never left Ajay's face, searching for tells, for the microscopic flinches that might reveal deception. "And you touched her head?"

The question was simple, but it carried the weight of condemnation. In the current climate of suspicion and fear, any physical contact between an adult and a child was viewed through the lens of potential abuse. The sacred bond between teacher and student had been poisoned by the very real horrors perpetrated by a few, casting suspicion on the innocent majority.

"Yes," Ajay said, his voice steady despite the tremor in his hands. "Gently. Like a father would. Like my own father did for me when I was confused or scared. I didn't realize that even affection is dangerous now. I didn't know that compassion had become a crime."

The bitterness in his voice was unmistakable. This was the world they had created—a world where teachers were afraid to console crying children, where every gesture of care was scrutinized for hidden motives, where the innocent paid the price for the guilty's sins.

Patil's expression softened slightly, perhaps recognizing the genuine anguish in Ajay's voice. His own voice lowered, taking on a more cautious tone. "Don't speak like that here, Mr. Sharma. We're not debating the state of society or the philosophy of parenting. We're managing panic. The school wants you gone—quietly, without noise. They're terrified of scandal, of media attention. I'm just the messenger in this particular tragedy."

The honesty was brutal but not unkind. Patil had seen enough of these cases to know that truth was often secondary to perception, that institutions cared more about their image than about justice for individuals. He was caught between duty and conscience, between the demands of his superiors and his own sense of what was right.

Ajay looked down at his lap, studying his hands as if they held the answers to questions he couldn't even formulate. His voice was barely audible when he spoke. "You're here to break me, not to hear me. This isn't about truth or justice. It's about convenience."

The words hung in the air like an accusation, but there was no anger in them—only a profound sadness that seemed to age him years in the space of moments. He had spent his entire life believing in the power of truth, in the fundamental goodness of human nature, in the idea that justice would ultimately prevail. Now, sitting in this station that reeked of compromise and expedience, those beliefs felt as fragile as autumn leaves.

A pause stretched between them, filled with the weight of mutual understanding. The ticking clock grew louder, each second marking the passage of time that could not be reclaimed. The weight of the moment pressed down on both men—one who had seen too many cases to believe in absolute truth, and another who was discovering that truth meant nothing when fear took the driver's seat.

Around them, the station continued its nocturnal rhythm. The weeping mother's sobs had subsided into quiet hiccups. The young man continued to stare at the floor as if it might open up and swallow him whole. The clerk continued his mechanical scribbling, each entry another small tragedy in the endless catalogue of human failing.

When Hope Walked In

Patil opened his mouth to reply, perhaps to offer some small comfort or to explain the harsh realities of the system they were both trapped in. But before he could speak, before he could add his voice to the symphony of institutional indifference, a firm voice echoed from the doorway like a thunderclap.

"I need to speak to Mr. Ajay Sharma. Now."

The words cut through the heavy atmosphere like a blade, sharp and decisive. Everyone in the waiting area turned toward the source of the voice, their various miseries momentarily forgotten in the face of this new development. Even the clerk looked up from his register, his pen paused mid-word.

Nandini stood in the threshold like a storm just about to break, her presence immediately commanding attention. Dressed in a navy-blue kurti that spoke of professional competence and faded jeans that suggested she had come in haste, her hair tied in a loose bun that had been disturbed by her rush through the night streets, she looked every bit the corporate woman who had learned to navigate the corridors of power.

But it was her eyes that held everyone's attention—they burned with a fire that spoke of old wounds and fierce determination. It was a fire Ajay recognized, one that had illuminated their shared dreams years ago. The same fire that had stood beside him when they defied their families to be together, that had fought alongside him through the early struggles of marriage, that had burned brightest during their brief, shining moment of parenthood.

It was also the fire that had died the day their daughter was taken from them, extinguished by grief too profound to bear. Seeing it again now, rekindled by crisis and compassion, was like seeing a ghost return to life.

Behind her stood a tall man in a crisp white shirt that somehow managed to look fresh despite the late hour, neatly ironed with military precision, carrying a leather briefcase that spoke of success and competence. There was an air of controlled calmness about him, the kind of composure that came from years of fighting battles in courtrooms where words were weapons and silence could be fatal. His eyes were already scanning the room like a hawk surveying its territory, cataloguing faces, assessing threats, calculating odds.

"This is Advocate Vikrant Shelar," Nandini said, her voice carrying the authority of someone accustomed to being heard. She flashed a business card toward Patil with the practiced efficiency of someone who had learned to navigate bureaucratic obstacles. "He represents Mr. Sharma."

The simple statement sent ripples through the waiting area. Suddenly, the dynamics had shifted. Ajay was no longer just another suspect being processed through the system's machinery. He was a man with representation, with someone willing to fight for him, someone who understood the language of law and procedure that governed this place.

Patil frowned, his earlier cooperative demeanour hardening into official resistance. "There's no FIR filed yet. No formal arrest has been made. No case has been registered. You can't claim legal representation in a non-existent case, madam."

His words carried the weight of protocol, the safety of established procedure. But there was something else in his tone—a recognition that the game had changed, that this would no longer be a simple matter of following orders and managing perceptions.

Vikrant stepped forward, his movements deliberate and

measured. His voice was even, professionally modulated, but there was steel beneath the silk. "That's exactly why we're here, Sub-Inspector. Before it becomes a case. Before you subject a respected educator to third-degree tactics. Before irreversible damage is done to a man whose only crime appears to be caring too much. Let's speak reasonably, like civilized people."

The tension in the room shifted palpably, like the change in atmospheric pressure before a storm. Suddenly, the power balance was different. The clerk had stopped his mechanical scribbling entirely, watching the confrontation with the fascination of someone witnessing a rare event. The constables exchanged glances, suddenly uncertain about their roles in this evolving drama.

Even the weeping mother looked up from her private misery, perhaps wondering if hope was still possible in this place where it seemed to have been systematically extinguished. The young man beside her raised his head for the first time, his eyes focusing on this new development with the desperation of someone grasping for any sign that the system might still contain some measure of justice.

Ajay stared at Nandini, his mind struggling to process her presence here, in this place that felt like the opposite of everything they had once shared. Four years of silence, four years of careful avoidance, four years of living separate lives in the same city—and now she was here, in his darkest hour, standing between him and the forces that sought to destroy him.

His lips barely moved as he spoke, his voice a whisper that carried the weight of years of unexpressed gratitude and regret. "You came… "

The simple words contained multitudes. They spoke of the surprise that anyone would care enough to fight for him, of the old connection that had somehow survived the devastating loss that had torn them apart, of the complex emotions that seeing her again had stirred in his chest like sediment in still water.

Nandini's composure cracked slightly at his words. She swallowed hard, her throat working as she struggled to maintain her professional facade. When she spoke, her voice was carefully controlled, but there was an undertone of pain that spoke of old wounds imperfectly healed. "For her. For Pallavi."

The name hung in the air between them like a bridge across the chasm of their separation. It was a name that connected past and present, loss and hope, the daughter they had lost and the daughter he had found. In that moment, the crowded police station faded away, and they were alone with their shared history and the child who had somehow become their unexpected link to each other.

Ajay's brows tightened with sudden concern, the parent in him overriding everything else. His voice carried the urgent worry of a father who had been separated from his child. "Pallavi? She's alone at home?"

The question revealed the depth of his love for the little girl, the way fatherhood had transformed him from a man dealing with his own crisis into someone whose primary concern was always the welfare of his child. Even here, in the midst of his own nightmare, his first thought was for her safety and comfort.

Nandini gave a soft nod, her expression gentle with understanding. "Don't worry. Natasha is with her. She's safe, she's comfortable, and she's probably fast asleep by now, dreaming of tomorrow's adventures."

The reassurance settled some of the tension in Ajay's shoulders, though the guilt of leaving his daughter remained etched in the lines around his eyes. He had always been there for her bedtime stories, for her midnight fears, for the simple comfort of knowing Papa was just in the next room. Tonight, for the first time since he had adopted her, he had failed to be there when she needed him.

Patil exhaled loudly; his frustration evident in the way his shoulders sagged. The arrival of legal representation had complicated what should have been a simple matter of institutional damage control. "Fine," he said, his voice carrying the weight of resignation. "You have five minutes. Use them wisely."

The concession was grudging, but it was enough. In the world of police stations and bureaucratic procedure, five minutes could be an eternity if used correctly. It was time to assess the situation, to understand the charges, to begin building a defence against accusations that could destroy a man's life.

The Side Room

They were led into a smaller chamber that served multiple functions—half interrogation room, half forgotten storeroom. The space spoke of institutional neglect and the casual cruelty of a system that processed human suffering with mechanical efficiency. A broken chair leaned against the wall like a wounded soldier, its missing leg a testament to the countless souls who had sat in it awaiting their fate.

Files were piled on a dusty table in haphazard stacks, their contents representing years of human drama reduced to paperwork and procedure. The air was thick with the smell of old paper and stale hope, creating an atmosphere that seemed to leach the life from anyone who entered. A tube light flickered above them like a nervous pulse, casting erratic shadows that made the room feel unstable, as if reality itself was uncertain.

The walls were painted in institutional green, a colour that might once have been chosen for its calming properties but now seemed to emphasize the sterile nature of justice reduced to bureaucracy. Water stains on the ceiling told stories of monsoons past, while the concrete floor bore the scuff marks of countless feet—some belonging to the innocent, others to the guilty, all of them human beings caught in the machinery of a system that rarely distinguished between the two.

Ajay sat on the edge of a wooden bench that had been worn smooth by years of use. The wood was dark with age and human contact, scarred by the nervous fidgeting of people facing the most difficult moments of their lives. His hands rested on his knees, fingers occasionally twitching as if he wanted to reach out and touch something real, something that would anchor him to the world he had known before this nightmare began.

Nandini stood by the door, her posture rigid with tension, arms crossed defensively across her chest. She seemed to be guarding not just the exit but also her own emotional state, maintaining the distance that had become second nature to her over the years of their separation. Her eyes moved constantly, taking in the details of the room, the positioning of the furniture, the subtle dynamics of power that played out in such spaces.

The silence stretched between them like a chasm that had been growing for four years, filled with unspoken words and unresolved emotions. Here they were, in the most unlikely of places, forced to confront not just the present crisis but the ghosts of their shared past. The flickering light cast strange shadows on their faces, transforming them in turns—making them look like strangers who had never shared a bed, never planned a future together, never held their dying daughter in their arms, and then like the young lovers they had once been, full of hope and certainty about their place in the world.

The room itself seemed to encourage confession, its stark walls and harsh lighting designed to strip away pretence and reveal truth. But the truth between Ajay and Nandini was complex, layered with years of pain and carefully maintained distance. They had become experts at avoiding each other, at living parallel lives in the same city, at pretending that the love they had once shared had never existed.

Vikrant, meanwhile, had positioned himself strategically near the table, his briefcase open and a legal pad ready. He was the buffer between them, the professional presence that made this reunion possible by giving it a legitimate purpose. His eyes moved between them with the practiced assessment of someone who had seen how personal relationships could complicate legal cases, how emotion could cloud judgment when clear thinking was most necessary.

Unspoken Words

Ajay broke the silence first, his voice carrying the weight of years of accumulated guilt and gratitude. "Thank you for coming. I wasn't sure you'd come. I wasn't sure you'd even care anymore."

The words hung in the air like a confession, revealing the depth of his isolation and the surprise he felt at this gesture of support. He had spent four years believing that he was alone in the world, that the bridges between him and his past had been burned beyond repair. Her presence here challenged that assumption, forcing him to reconsider everything he thought he knew about their relationship.

Nandini's expression remained carefully neutral, but there was a flicker of something—pain, perhaps, or regret—in her eyes. Her voice when she spoke was controlled, professional, but there was an undertone of accusation that spoke of old wounds that had never properly healed. "You didn't call me in four years, Ajay. Not once. Not even when you adopted her. Not even when you needed help. Why now?"

The question was fair, but it cut deep. It spoke to the complexity of their separation, to the way grief had driven them apart when they should have been drawing closer together. It revealed the hurt she had carried, the feeling of abandonment that had grown with each passing year of silence.

Ajay's response was quiet, introspective, heavy with the weight of decisions made in pain and regret. "I didn't know how to bridge the gap between us. After everything that happened, after the way we fell apart, it didn't feel right to reach out. You had your life, your career, your new beginning. I had mine. I thought it was better to leave things as they were."

The explanation was honest but inadequate. How could he express the complexity of his feelings—the way he had wanted to call her a thousand times, the way he had drafted messages that were never sent, the way he had driven past her office just to catch a glimpse of her life without him? How could he explain that his silence had been an act of love, a recognition that they had both needed space to heal?

She stepped forward slightly, her carefully maintained composure cracking just enough to reveal the emotion beneath. Her voice was softer now, more vulnerable. "But you named her Pallavi."

The observation was simple, but it carried the weight of recognition. In choosing that name, Ajay had revealed that he had never truly moved on, that the daughter they had lost continued to live in his heart. It was a gesture of remembrance that spoke louder than any words could have.

Ajay nodded slowly, his voice caught somewhere between his throat and his heart. "I couldn't name her anything else. When I saw her, alone and scared, something inside me recognized her. It felt like... she chose the name herself. Like she was meant to carry it."

The admission hung in the air like a prayer, revealing the spiritual dimension of his connection to the child he had rescued. In his mind, perhaps, the two 'Pallavi's were connected—the one they had lost and the one he had found, both precious, both deserving of love and protection.

Nandini's eyes welled up with tears that she fought to contain. Her voice was barely a whisper when she spoke. "Is she really an orphan? Do you know anything about her family?"

The question revealed her own complex feelings about the child who bore their daughter's name. Part of her needed to know if there was someone else out there who had a claim to this little girl, someone who might have the right to take her away from the man who had become her father.

Ajay's response was immediate and firm, carrying the conviction of someone who had wrestled with these questions himself. "I found her near the market, during the monsoon. She was alone, hungry, scared. I tried to walk past—God forgive me, I tried to mind my own business. But something stopped me. She looked at me with such trust, such hope. I couldn't abandon her. I did what I had to do."

The story was simple, but it revealed the kind of man Ajay had become—someone who couldn't walk away from suffering, even when it meant complicating his own life. It spoke to the core of his character, the gentle strength that had made him a beloved teacher and a devoted father.

The words hung in the air like a confession, revealing not just the circumstances of Pallavi's adoption but the kind of man Ajay had remained despite the tragedies that had shaped him. He was still the person who couldn't ignore a child in need, who would risk his own comfort and security to ensure that someone else was safe.

Nandini understood this about him. She always had. It was one of the qualities that had drawn her to him in the first place—his instinctive compassion, his inability to turn away from suffering, his belief that every person deserved dignity and care. Seeing it still intact, still driving his decisions even in the face of potential consequences, reminded her of the man she had fallen in love with so many years ago.

There was silence again, but it wasn't hostile anymore. It was the quiet of wounds resurfacing, of shared memories being acknowledged, of two people who had loved each other deeply beginning to remember what that love had felt like. The flickering light above them seemed to steady slightly, as if the room itself was responding to the shift in emotional atmosphere.

The Reality Check

Vikrant cleared his throat softly, a gentle reminder that they were not alone and that the immediate crisis required their attention. His voice was professional but not unkind. "Let's focus on the present situation. The principal tried to handle this quietly, which actually helps our case. But if a formal complaint is filed, if this becomes public, we need to act quickly and decisively. The media can flip this story either way—you could be portrayed as a dedicated teacher being persecuted for showing normal human compassion, or as a predator who used his position to exploit vulnerable children."

The stark assessment brought them back to the harsh reality of their situation. In the court of public opinion, nuance was often lost, and the complexity of human relationships was reduced to simple narratives that served the media's need for drama and sensation.

Patil re-entered the room at that moment, his expression grim but not entirely unsympathetic. He had been a police officer long enough to recognize the difference between genuine monsters and decent people caught in impossible situations. His voice carried the weariness of someone who had seen too much of both.

"No formal charges yet," he said, his words offering a small measure of hope. "But the pressure is building like steam in a kettle. School trustees are nervous about their reputation. The education board is asking questions. And yes—the media's already sniffing around. One of the local reporters got wind of the story and has been making calls."

The mention of media attention sent a visible shiver through

Ajay's body. He had seen how quickly public opinion could turn, how a single headline could destroy a lifetime of careful work and dedicated service. In today's connected world, where information spread faster than wildfire and context was often lost in the rush to judgment, accusation was tantamount to conviction, especially when it involved the safety of children.

The thought of his name being splashed across newspaper headlines, of his photograph being shared on social media alongside accusations of impropriety, of Pallavi potentially seeing or hearing about these things—it was almost too much to bear. He had always been a private person, someone who preferred to do his good work quietly, without fanfare or recognition. The idea of being thrust into the spotlight for all the wrong reasons was a special kind of torment.

Nandini stepped forward, her voice carrying the authority of someone who had mastered the art of handling boardroom intrigue and managing public perception. Her tone was firm, brooking no argument. "Then don't make a mistake you'll regret, Sub-Inspector. Let Ajay go home tonight. Let him return to his daughter, who needs him now more than ever. If there's anything further to discuss, we'll respond through proper legal channels."

The demand was reasonable but delivered with the confidence of someone who expected to be taken seriously. he had learned, through years of professional experience, how to project authority even when she felt uncertain inside.

Patil hesitated, running a hand over his forehead in a gesture that spoke of the pressures he faced from multiple directions. He had superiors who wanted this handled quietly, a school administration that wanted the problem to disappear, and now a lawyer who was threatening to make everything more complicated if proper procedures weren't followed.

"Fine," he said finally, his voice carrying the weight of compromise. "But I'll need a written assurance that he won't leave the city. And if we need to speak with him again, he needs to be available immediately."

"Done," Vikrant said, already pulling a notepad from his briefcase with practiced efficiency. "I'll draft the undertaking right now."

As Vikrant began to write, Ajay found himself looking at Nandini again, really looking at her for the first time since she had arrived. The years had changed her, as they had changed him. There were lines around her eyes that spoke of stress and responsibility, a set to her shoulders that suggested she had learned to carry burdens alone. But there was also something familiar about her presence, something that awakened memories of the partnership they had once shared.

There were so many words unspoken between them, so many conversations that had been avoided, so many feelings that had been buried beneath the necessity of moving forward. Regret hung in the air like incense, mixed with relief and perhaps, somewhere deep down, the first tentative spark of something that might eventually become reconciliation.

As Vikrant continued to scribble the legal undertaking, Ajay caught Nandini's eye and held it for a moment. For just an instant, they weren't in a police station surrounded by the debris of broken lives and institutional indifference. They were young again, planning their future together, believing that love could conquer any obstacle, that their partnership could weather any storm.

The moment passed, as such moments always do, but something had shifted between them. A door that had been locked for four years had creaked open, just a fraction. Not enough to walk through, perhaps, but enough to let in a sliver of light, a whisper of possibility that the future might hold something other than the careful avoidance they had practiced for so long.

Home

The key turned in the lock with a soft click that seemed to echo through the quiet neighbourhood. Ajay stepped into his home just past midnight, the familiar scent of the small apartment wrapping around him like an embrace. The house was quiet, bathed in the gentle glow of a single lamp that cast warm shadows across the modest furniture he had chosen with care over the years.

Near the sofa, little Pallavi lay asleep in a position that spoke of a child's complete abandon to rest. Her tiny fingers were curled around a stuffed elephant that had been her constant companion since the day he had brought her home—a grey creature with floppy ears and a gentle expression that seemed to understand the weight of being a child's primary confidant.

Her dark hair spread across the cushion like silk, and her breathing was steady and peaceful, unmarked by the anxiety that had consumed her earlier in the evening. She had changed into her favourite pyjamas—the ones with tiny stars scattered across a deep blue background that made her look like she was sleeping under the night sky itself.

Her small shoes were neatly arranged beside the doormat, placed there with the careful precision that he had taught her over months of patient instruction. It was one of those small victories of parenting that other people might overlook, but which filled him with quiet pride every time he saw it. In a world that had shown her chaos and abandonment, she had learned to find comfort in order and routine.

A drawing book lay half-open on the floor nearby, its pages filled with the colourful artwork that had become her way of processing the world around her. He could see the edge of a picture she had been working on—what looked like a house with a garden, stick figures that probably represented the two of them, and a sun that took up nearly a quarter of the page with its enthusiastic yellow rays.

The scene was so perfectly domestic, so beautifully ordinary, that it made his chest tighten with emotion. This was what he had been fighting for in that sterile police station—not just his own reputation or freedom, but the right to continue being the father this little girl needed, the right to preserve the safe harbour they had built together against the storms of an uncertain world.

Natasha sat in the armchair beside the sofa, her legs tucked under her in a position that suggested she had been there for hours. She was leafing through a children's storybook—one of the many that lined the small bookshelf Ajay had built when Pallavi first came to live with them. The book was "Where the Wild Things Are," and he could see that several pages had been dog-eared from repeated readings.

When she looked up as Ajay entered, her eyes held a mixture of relief and concern. For the first time since he had known her, there was no judgment in her gaze, no subtle criticism of his choices or his lifestyle. Instead, there was something that looked almost like respect, as if the events of the evening had shown her a side of him that she had never seen before.

"She kept asking where you were," Natasha said softly, her voice barely above a whisper so as not to wake the sleeping child. "I told her you had some work to finish at school, but I think she knew something was wrong. Children have a way of sensing these things, don't they?"

Her words carried the weight of someone who was beginning to understand the depth of the bond between father and daughter, the way they had learned to read each other's moods and needs through the countless small interactions that made up their daily life together.

Ajay whispered back, his voice heavy with guilt and

exhaustion, "She's too young to understand any of this. She shouldn't have to worry about whether Papa is coming home."

The simple statement revealed the core of his anguish—not just the threat to his own life and reputation, but the knowledge that his troubles would inevitably touch the innocent child who depended on him completely. He had worked so hard to create a world of safety and predictability for her, and now that world was under assault from forces she couldn't comprehend.

Understanding

"I understand now," Nandini said quietly from her position near the window, where she had been standing silently since they arrived. Her voice carried a note of discovery, as if she had been putting together pieces of a puzzle that had been scattered for years.

Ajay looked at her, studying the way the lamplight played across her features, highlighting the changes that time had wrought while somehow emphasizing the essential qualities that had remained constant. She looked older, more mature, marked by experiences he had not shared. But there was something in her expression that reminded him of the woman he had fallen in love with—a capacity for empathy that had always been one of her most beautiful qualities.

"What do you understand?" he asked, genuinely curious about the thoughts that had been forming in her mind as she watched him interact with his adopted daughter.

She turned from the window; her silhouette framed against the soft glow of the street lamps outside. When she spoke, her voice was soft but clear, carrying the weight of realization. "I understand that you didn't just adopt a child. You found a way to heal, to channel your love into something that could grow and flourish. You found a way to be a father again."

The observation was simple but profound. She had recognized something that he himself had only recently begun to understand—that his decision to adopt Pallavi had been about more than just rescuing a child in need. It had been about reclaiming a part of himself that had been lost, about finding a way to love again after devastating loss.

He moved slowly to the sofa, his steps careful and deliberate so as not to disturb the sleeping child. Kneeling beside her, he brushed a strand of hair away from her forehead with the gentle touch of someone who had learned to be tender through practice and intention. She stirred slightly at his touch but didn't wake, instead settling deeper into sleep with the unconscious trust of a child who knew she was safe.

The gesture was automatic, born of countless similar moments over the years they had been together. It was the kind of parental intimacy that develops gradually, through bedtime stories and comfort after nightmares, through scraped knees and proud moments at school functions. It was exactly the kind of innocent, loving touch that had been twisted into something sinister by fearful minds and institutional paranoia.

Nandini watched this interaction silently, her trained eye noting the natural ease with which he moved around the child, the way his entire demeanour softened in her presence. There was nothing forced or calculated about his movements—they carried the unconscious grace of someone who had learned to love through action rather than words, who had discovered that parenthood was less about grand gestures and more about the accumulation of small, tender moments.

A moment passed, heavy with the weight of shared history and the complex emotions that seeing him as a father again had stirred within her. In the dim light of the living room, she could see the man she had once loved—gentle, protective, full of quiet strength that never needed to announce itself. The years had aged him, carved lines around his eyes and threaded silver through his hair, but his essence remained unchanged. He was still the man who would stop to help a stranger, who would give his last rupee to someone in need, who would risk his own reputation to save a child.

The realization hit her like a physical blow—not painful, but profound. She had spent four years carefully constructing a life without him, building walls around her heart to protect herself from the memories of what they had lost together. But seeing him now, in his element as a father, she understood that some connections transcend time and circumstance, that some bonds are too deep to be severed by grief or distance.

"You've become exactly the father you always dreamed of being," she said softly, her voice carrying a note of wonder mixed with an old, familiar pain. "Even after everything we lost, you found a way to love again."

Her words hung in the air like a blessing and a recognition. She was acknowledging not just his success as a parent, but his courage in choosing to risk his heart again after it had been so completely shattered. It took a special kind of strength to remain open to love after experiencing such devastating loss.

Ajay looked up from Pallavi's sleeping form, his eyes meeting Nandini's across the small distance that separated them. For a moment, the years fell away, and they were the young couple who had dreamed of having children together, who had made plans and shared hopes for the family they would create.

"I had to," he said simply, his voice barely above a whisper. "I couldn't let the darkness win. I couldn't let our loss mean that I would never love a child again. When I found her, it felt like... like I was being given a second chance to do what I was meant to do."

The admission was raw, honest, revealing the spiritual

dimension of his connection to Pallavi. He had seen her adoption not as a replacement for what he had lost, but as a continuation of his journey as a father, a way of honouring the love he had felt for their daughter by extending it to another child who needed it desperately.

The Promise

She set down her bag, her movements deliberate as she made a decision that surprised even herself. The evening had been emotionally exhausting for all of them, filled with revelations and reconciliations that would take time to process. But there was something different about her now, a softness that hadn't been there when she arrived at the police station.

"I'm staying tonight," she said, her voice carrying a promise that went beyond mere legal assistance. "Pallavi shouldn't be alone, and neither should you when you return. We'll talk more in the morning. There's so much we need to discuss- about the case, about Pallavi, about... everything."

The last word carried the weight of their shared history, the unfinished conversations and unresolved emotions that had been stirred up by the evening's events. They both knew that this crisis had opened doors that had been carefully locked for years, that there would be no returning to the careful avoidance they had practiced for so long.

Ajay stood slowly; his movements careful not to disturb the sleeping child. When he spoke, his voice carried a vulnerability that she remembered from their early days together. "Will you help me fight this? I can't do it alone, and I'm scared of what this could mean for her."

The question revealed the depth of his fear- not just for himself, but for the innocent child who depended on him completely. He had always been someone who preferred to handle his problems independently, who found it difficult to ask for help even when he desperately needed it. The fact that he was reaching out now spoke to the gravity of the situation and the trust he still placed in her judgment.

She moved closer to him, the lamplight catching her face at just the right angle, highlighting the determination in her eyes and the set of her jaw that indicated she had made a decision that would not be easily changed.

"Yes," she whispered, the single word carrying the weight of renewed partnership and shared purpose. "I'll help you fight this. For her, for you, for... for all of us."

The promise was simple but comprehensive. She was committing not just to legal assistance, but to emotional support, to standing beside him as he faced the challenges that lay ahead. It was a return to the partnership they had once shared, transformed by loss and time but still fundamentally strong.

New Beginnings

As Natasha stepped into the lift, the metallic doors sliding shut with a quiet finality, Ajay nodded his gratitude from the doorway. She had stayed to help during the crisis, but now it was time for her to return to her own life. He watched the floor indicator descend until she was gone, then closed the door softly.

As the hours passed and Pallavi settled into peaceful sleep, Ajay and Nandini found themselves in the kitchen, the same space where they had once shared countless conversations over cups of tea. The familiar ritual of making tea together felt both strange and natural, their movements around each other careful but gradually more comfortable.

For the first time in four years, he didn't feel completely alone. The road ahead would be treacherous, filled with legal battles and public scrutiny that could destroy everything he had built. The media attention would be intense, and the court of public opinion could be cruel and unforgiving. But he wouldn't have to walk that difficult path alone.

The woman who had once been his partner in all things had returned, not as a lover or a wife, but as an ally in the fight for his daughter's future and his own redemption. It wasn't the reunion he had sometimes dreamed of in his loneliest moments, but it was something precious nonetheless- a restoration of trust and mutual respect that had seemed impossible just hours before.

"I've been thinking about what comes next," she said, her voice low to avoid waking Pallavi. "Vikrant will handle the legal aspects, but we need to think about the broader implications. The school board, the media, the community- they all need to see who you really are."

Ajay nodded, grateful for her strategic thinking. "The truth will come out eventually. It has to."

"Yes, but we can't just wait for it to emerge on its own. We need to be proactive, to tell your story before others distort it beyond recognition."

They talked until the early hours of the morning, their conversation ranging from immediate practical concerns to longer-term implications. The intimacy of the moment wasn't romantic- it was something deeper, the intimacy of two people who had loved each other deeply and were now choosing to trust each other again in the face of extraordinary circumstances.

When exhaustion finally overtook them, she settled on the couch with a pillow and blanket, while he remained in the chair beside Pallavi's room, unwilling to leave his daughter's side. Tomorrow would bring new challenges, new accusations, new battles to fight. The school board would want answers, the media would want statements, and the legal system would want proof of innocence in a society that seemed increasingly willing to assume guilt.

But tonight, in the quiet sanctuary of his home, with his daughter sleeping peacefully nearby and the promise of support from the woman who had once been his everything, he allowed himself a moment of peace.

The clock on the wall ticked steadily forward, marking the passage of time that could not be reclaimed. But for once, Ajay wasn't afraid of what the next moment might bring. He had faced the darkness of accusation and suspicion and emerged still standing, still fighting, still believing in the power of truth and love to overcome even the most difficult circumstances.

Whatever lay ahead, he would face it with the same quiet courage that had carried him through the worst moments of his life. He would fight for his daughter's right to grow up in a world where love was not automatically suspect, where kindness was not immediately questioned, where a father's gentle touch was recognized as the blessing it was meant to be.

The story was far from over. In fact, as he sat there in the lamplight, watching over the sleeping child who had given his life new meaning and purpose, he realized that in many ways, it was just beginning. The real test would come not in police stations or courtrooms, but in the daily act of continuing to love and protect and nurture, regardless of what the world might say or think.

The night settled around them like a protective embrace, and for the first time in hours, Ajay Sharma allowed himself to believe that tomorrow might bring not just challenges, but hope. Outside, the city continued its restless sleep, but inside this small apartment, time seemed to slow and soften, creating a pocket of peace in the midst of chaos- a family reunited by crisis, strengthened by shared purpose, ready to face whatever storms lay ahead.

Chapter 4: The Fire Spreads

The court of Public Opinion

By dawn, the whispers had become headlines. "Primary School Teacher Accused of Inappropriate Conduct with Minor." "Vidya Vihar Scandal: Silence in the Classrooms, Questions in the Streets." "City's Top School Under Fire—Are Our Children Safe?"

Television anchors raised their voices in carefully rehearsed outrage. Social media posts erupted with judgment, condemnation, and fury. WhatsApp forwards spun wild theories, adding layers of imaginary horror and false details. A parent had spoken, and now the city was not just listening—it was roaring.

The digital wildfire had consumed everything in its path. Facebook posts multiplied like viruses, each sharing adding another layer of distortion. Twitter hashtags trended with venomous certainty—'Justice for Children', 'Arrest the Monster', 'School Shame. You Tube videos dissected every angle with clickbait thumbnails showing Ajay's grainy photograph circled in red. The comment sections became cesspools of rage, where strangers competed to express the most righteous fury.

In coffee shops and bus stops, in office corridors and residential societies, Ajay's name was whispered with the same disgust reserved for confirmed criminals. The court of public opinion had convened, deliberated, and delivered its verdict before the sun had fully risen.

Ajay woke up to the buzz of his phone. Twenty missed calls blinked accusingly from the screen—unknown numbers, perhaps reporters or old acquaintances pretending to care. The press had begun their hunt. He walked to the window, the glass reflecting a man he barely recognized. His own face blurred into the orange-pink skyline as the first rays of sun broke over the city.

The morning light felt different today—harsh, unforgiving. It illuminated every crack in the apartment walls, every dust mote floating in the air, every imperfection he had never noticed before. Even the familiar sounds of the waking neighbourhood seemed alien now— children's laughter carried a mocking edge, the vegetable vendor's call sounded like an accusation, and the distant honking of traffic became a symphony of judgment.

From the next room came a soft yawn. Pallavi stirred, her small arms stretching like sunflower petals. Oblivious to the storm gathering outside, she murmured, "Daddy… is it school time?"

Ajay didn't reply. He just smiled faintly and closed the curtains.

In the kitchen, Nandini stood silently, pouring tea into two mismatched cups—the same blue-rimmed ones they had bought together from a street vendor during their honeymoon. She had stayed overnight, sleeping awkwardly on the wooden chair, her neck sore but her resolve firm. The kitchen smelled of over-boiled ginger and the lingering warmth of shared memories.

As the amber liquid streamed from the kettle, memories flooded back like a gentle tide. She remembered mornings when these same cups had held laughter along with tea, when their small kitchen had been filled with the music of their love. Ajay would appear behind her like a shadow made of warmth, his arms wrapping around her waist as she stood at the stove, his chin resting on her shoulder.

"Perfect blend," he would whisper against her ear, his breath sending shivers down her spine. "Just like you."

She would lean back into his embrace, feeling the steady rhythm of his heartbeat against her back. "You say that every morning," she would tease, her hands covering his as they rested on her waist.

"Because it's true every morning," he would reply, pressing a soft kiss to the curve of her neck. "My beautiful wife makes the tastiest tea."

Those morning rituals had been sacred to them. Before the world woke up, before responsibilities called, they had those precious moments when it was just the two of them in their small universe. He would tell her about his dreams from the night before—always gentle dreams of their future together, of the children they would have, of the little house they would buy someday with a garden where she could grow jasmine.

"I dreamed we were old," he had whispered one morning, his voice still thick with sleep. "Your hair was silver like moonlight, and you still made tea for me every morning."

"And did you still tell me it was perfect?" she had asked, turning in his arms to face him.

"Every single morning," he had promised, cupping her face in his hands. "Even when my memory fails, even when I forget everything else, I'll remember that you are my perfect blend."

She remembered how he would steal sips from her cup when she wasn't looking, claiming that tea tasted better when it was hers. When she would catch him, he would grin like a mischievous child, tea drops glistening on his lips.

"Thief," she would accuse, but her eyes would be dancing with affection.

"Guilty," he would admit, pulling her close. "I'm addicted to everything that's yours."

She would lean in and slowly lick the tea drops from his lips—claiming her stolen sip in the most delicious way.

She remembered Sunday mornings when they would linger in the kitchen, him reading the newspaper aloud while she prepared breakfast. He would pause dramatically at funny headlines, making her laugh until she couldn't breathe. When she would cook, he would be her willing assistant, chopping vegetables with exaggerated precision, humming old songs that made her heart dance.

"You're going to cut yourself," she would warn, watching him gesture enthusiastically with the knife.

"Then you'll have to take care of me," he would reply with a wink. "Kiss it better."

"Is that your plan? Injure yourself for kisses?"

"I don't need to injure myself for kisses from you," he would say, abandoning the vegetables to pull her into his arms. "I just need to ask."

And she would kiss him then, tasting the sweetness of his smile, feeling the warmth of his love surrounding her like the most beautiful cocoon.

The memory of their first Diwali in this kitchen made her smile despite everything. They had been so young, so hopeful, so utterly convinced that love could conquer anything. She had been trying to make sweets for the festival, failing spectacularly at her mother's recipes.

"They're supposed to be round," she had said, staring at the misshapen ladoos (small ball shaped Indian sweet dish made up of either semolina or gram flour) with dismay.

"They're perfect," Ajay had declared, picking up one of the lopsided sweets. "They're made with love."

"They're made with frustration and confusion," she had corrected. "Same thing," he had said, taking a bite. His face had contorted slightly—they were definitely too sweet—but he had smiled anyway. "Delicious."

"Liar."

"Lucky man," he had corrected, pulling her flour-dusted hands into his. "I'm married to a woman who cares enough to make sweets for me, even when they don't turn out exactly right."

They had ended up ordering sweets from the market, but not before he had kissed the flour from her nose, the sugar from her fingers, the disappointment from her lips.

She remembered the morning she had been sick with fever, how he had brought her tea in bed, sitting beside her and stroking her hair until she felt better. His touch had been so gentle, so reverent, like she was something precious that needed to be protected.

"I should make my own tea," she had protested weakly.

"Shh," he had whispered. "Let me take care of you. It's what husbands are for."

"I thought husbands were for reaching high shelves and killing spiders."

"Those too," he had agreed with a soft chuckle. "But mostly for loving you when you're sick, holding you when you're sad, and making you laugh when you're grumpy."

"I'm not grumpy."

"The grumpiest," he had said affectionately. "And I love you more for it."

The memory of their last good morning together rose unbidden—before the arguments started, before the disappointments crept in, before the world convinced her that gentle love wasn't enough. They had made tea together, moving around each other in the small kitchen like dancers who had practiced their steps for years.

"We should get a bigger kitchen someday," she had said, watching him reach around her for the sugar.

"Why? Then I wouldn't have an excuse to get this close to you while you're cooking," he had replied, his arm brushing against hers as he sweetened his tea.

"You don't need an excuse," she had assured him.

"I know," he had said, setting down his cup to frame her face with his hands. "But I like having one anyway."

He had kissed her then, soft and sweet, like a blessing for the day ahead. She had tasted the future in that kiss—years of mornings just like this one, decades of small intimacies, a lifetime of choosing each other every single day.

"If only she had known it would be the last of so many such mornings……… If only she had held onto the moment a little longer, memorized the way his hands felt against her skin, the way his eyes crinkled when he smiled, the way he said her name like it was a prayer……….. They had shared countless sunrises just like it—but this one, she would later realize, was the last. And some mornings only live once—leaving behind the ache of what could have been."

Now, as she stood in the same kitchen, pouring tea into the same blue-rimmed cups, she could feel the ghost of his presence behind her. For just a moment, she could almost feel his arms around her waist, his voice whispering against her ear, his love surrounding her like the most beautiful dream.

The steam from the tea rose like incense, carrying with it the essence of what they had once been—two people who had loved each other with the kind of pure, uncomplicated devotion that believed in happy endings. Before the world had taught them that love wasn't always enough, before life had shown them that sometimes the gentlest hearts were the most vulnerable to breaking.

A tear dropped into her cup filled with tea, and she realized she was crying—not from sadness, but from the overwhelming beauty of remembering what it felt like to be completely, utterly loved. Ajay had given her that gift, had shown her what it meant to be cherished, to be seen, to be valued not for what she could become but for who she already was.

She wiped her eyes and sipped the tea, her hands steady despite the emotions swirling through her heart. These memories weren't just remnants of the past—they were proof of the man Ajay truly was, the man she had been blessed to love and foolish enough to leave.

But now she was here, in his kitchen, sipping tea, fighting for the chance to create new memories, fighting for the chance to love him the way he had always deserved to be loved—completely, unconditionally, forever.

The tea was perfect, she realized. Just the right blend, just the right sweetness. Just the way he had always said it was, every single morning of their marriage.

Some things, she thought, were worth remembering. Some loves were worth fighting for and some men were worth saving, no matter what the world believed about them.

Ajay took the tea without a word, his fingers wrapping around the familiar blue rim. For a moment, she wondered if he remembered these cups too, if he was thinking about the same mornings she was. But his expression gave nothing away.

The tea tasted bitter to him, though she had added sugar—two spoons, just the way he liked it. She still remembered, despite everything. Everything felt bitter now—the morning air, the familiar walls, even the sunlight streaming through the small kitchen window.

They stood in silence, two people who had once planned a life together, now united only by crisis and the sleeping child in the next room. "Do you remember," she said suddenly, surprising herself, "when we first moved here? You said this kitchen was too small for two people to work in."

Ajay glanced at her, a faint smile touching his lips. "And you said we'd just have to learn to dance around each other."

"We did, for a while."

"Yes. We did."

The silence stretched between them, filled with the weight of all the things they had wanted but never said to each other, all the apologies that had come too late, all the love that had been buried under pride and disappointment.

"You're all over the news," she said quietly, her voice steadier than she felt. "There's a van with media outside. There are at least three men with cameras."

He nodded; gaze distant. "They want a headline, not the truth." Before they could delve deeper into dangerous territory, there was a knock on the door.

The Bureaucracy of Betrayal

Ajay froze, the cup half-raised. Nandini stepped forward cautiously. It wasn't the police this time. It was Raghu Desai, the school's administrative head, flanked by two senior staff members. All three looked like they had aged overnight—faces drawn with exhaustion and the particular kind of stress that came from being caught between loyalty and self-preservation.

Raghu looked uncomfortable as he entered, eyes avoiding Ajay's. Behind him, Ms. Kulkarni from the primary section shifted nervously, her usually cheerful demeanour replaced by professional distance. Mr. Patwardhan from administration stood like a reluctant executioner, the man who had once borrowed money from Ajay for his father's medical treatment now unable to meet his eyes.

"Ajay… we need to talk," Raghu said, his tone flat, rehearsed.

"Is this about my resignation again?" Ajay asked, already knowing the answer.

Raghu sighed, glancing at the others. The weight of institutional pressure was written across his features. He had been a teacher himself once, before climbing the administrative ladder. He understood the sacred trust between teacher and student, the devastation of false accusations. But he also understood the realities of running a school in the age of social media trials.

"Look, the school is facing intense pressure. Sponsors, trustees, parents—they're all demanding action. We suspended you this morning. Official notice is being served."

The words hung in the air like a death sentence. Ajay had expected this, but hearing it aloud felt like a physical blow. Twelve years of dedication, of staying late to help struggling students, of spending his own money on classroom supplies, of treating every child like his own—all of it erased with a few administrative sentences.

"Without a hearing? Without proof?" Ajay's voice was steady, but Nandini could see the pain in his eyes.

"We've received formal instructions from the management. We'll cooperate with the inquiry, but in the meantime, you're not to set foot on school grounds."

Ms. Kulkarni finally spoke, her voice barely above a whisper. "Ajay, we... we don't believe the allegations. But our hands are tied."

She remembered how he had stayed after hours to help her son Rohit with mathematics when the boy was struggling. How he had patiently explained fractions using chocolate bars and cricket scores until the concepts clicked. How he had refused any payment, saying that helping children was never a burden.

Mr. Patwardhan's guilt was written across his face. Two years ago, when his father had suffered a heart attack, Ajay had admitted him to the hospital and deposited the initial payment in cash. The money had covered the hospital deposit that insurance wouldn't cover. Now, he was part of the team destroying the same man who had shown him such kindness.

"The board met in emergency session," Raghu continued, his voice growing more strained. "They're concerned about the school's reputation. Enrolment for next year might be affected. Three corporate sponsors have threatened to withdraw funding."

Ajay nodded slowly, understanding the brutal calculus of institutional survival. He had seen it before—when the previous principal had been forced to resign over a minor scandal, when the Sanskrit teacher had been let go for being too old, when the music teacher had been terminated for being too progressive. Schools were businesses first, educational institutions second. Teachers were expendable resources, easily replaced when they became inconvenient.

"I understand," he said quietly. "You're protecting the school."

"We're protecting the future of eight hundred children," Raghu said, but his voice lacked conviction.

Nandini stepped between them, her voice sharp as a blade. "You do realize this is feeding the media frenzy, don't you? You're throwing him under the bus to protect your image."

Raghu glanced at her, trying to maintain what little dignity remained. "This is not personal, Ms.—"

"Deshmukh," she said firmly, using her maiden name. "And it is personal. He's my ex-husband. And the father of a child who just watched two policemen take him away."

The temperature in the room seemed to drop. Raghu's face fell as the full weight of the situation hit him. This wasn't just about a teacher and allegations—there was a child involved, a daughter who would suffer for her father's persecution.

Ms. Kulkarni's eyes moistened. She had children of her own, understood the particular cruelty of watching a parent be taken away by authorities. Mr. Patwardhan's eyes also grew moist, his hands fidgeting with the official documents they had brought.

"Look," Raghu said, his voice softer now, "if this whole thing blows over, if the allegations are proven false, we'll... we'll consider reinstatement."

"Consider?" Nandini's voice could have cut glass. "After destroying his reputation, after abandoning him when he needed support most, you'll consider giving him back his life?"

"We're doing what we must," Raghu said, placing a printed letter on the dining table. The official school letterhead looked strange and hostile now, like a weapon disguised as correspondence. "Good day."

Raghu's voice grew more strained as he continued. "There's something else you should know, Ajay. After the board meeting, Principal Joshi submitted her resignation. She said she couldn't continue in a position where she was forced to abandon a teacher without due process."

Mr. Patwardhan shifted uncomfortably, finally finding his voice. "We... all three of us submitted our resignations yesterday. We couldn't be part of this injustice. But the principal wouldn't accept our resignations," Ms. Kulkarni added quietly, her voice heavy with guilt. "She said the students needed stability, that we couldn't all abandon ship. She's temporarily assuming the principal's duties until..." "Until what?" Ajay asked, though he already knew the answer. Raghu met his eyes directly for the first time since entering. "Until the management makes alternate arrangements. She said she'll only return to her position when you're back.

"The revelation hung in the air like a heavy weight. Even in her compromise with institutional pressure, Ms. Joshi had found a way to express her faith in Ajay's innocence. It was a gesture that spoke louder than any formal support could have.

Ajay and Nandini felt sorry for the harsh thoughts that had initially crossed their minds when all three of them conveyed the management's decision.

The door closed behind them with a finality that seemed to echo through the apartment. Silence returned. Thicker than before, heavy with the weight of betrayal and institutional cowardice.

Ajay exhaled slowly, picking up the letter. "It's begun."

The words blurred together as he read—"suspension pending inquiry," "serious allegations," "school's reputation," "immediate effect." Bureaucratic language that reduced a man's life to administrative convenience, that transformed twelve years of dedication into a liability to be managed.

He folded the letter carefully, his hands steady despite the storm raging inside him. "They're right, you know. They have to protect the school."

"Don't you dare defend them," Nandini said fiercely. "You gave them everything. Your time, your energy, your own money. You made that school better, and now they're discarding you like garbage."

"They're afraid," Ajay said simply. "And now I understand they're suffering too. Fear makes good people do terrible things."

The Media Circus

Outside the building, the media presence had grown. What had started as a few curious reporters had evolved into a full-scale circus. Television vans lined the street, their satellite dishes pointed skyward like technological prayer wheels. Reporters practiced their opening lines, cameramen tested their equipment, and photographers adjusted their lenses for the perfect shot of justice in action.

Ajay stood at the window, watching the spectacle with fascination and horror. He recognized some faces from the local news—the crime reporter from Channel 7 who had covered the previous year's education scandal, the young journalist from the morning show who specialized in social issues. They stood in clusters, sharing information, building narratives, preparing to broadcast judgment to thousands of viewers.

In their minds, he realized, he was already guilty. The story was too perfect, too aligned with society's anxieties about child safety, to be questioned. A male teacher, a vulnerable student, a prestigious school—all the elements were there for a narrative that would capture attention and drive ratings.

He thought about the dreams he had harboured, the fantasies of recognition and appreciation that had sustained him through years of underappreciation. How different this attention was from what he had imagined.

In his dreams, the media had come to celebrate him. He had pictured himself standing before microphones, humble but proud, as reporters asked him about his work with disadvantaged children. He had imagined the headlines: "Teacher's Selfless Act Saves Child," "Modern Day Hero Gives Street Child New Life," "From Abandonment to Achievement: One Man's Mission."

The dream had been so vivid he could almost taste it. Cameras flashing as he told Pallavi's story—how he had found her abandoned, how he had fought the system to adopt her, how he had given her not just a home but a future. The grateful tears in the interviewer's eyes as he explained his philosophy of education, his belief that every child deserved a chance regardless of their background.

He had imagined Pallavi beside him, shy but proud, as he spoke about her transformation from a frightened, abandoned child to a confident, loving daughter. The audience would have been moved by her resilience, inspired by his dedication. They would have seen him as he truly as—not a saint, but a man who had chosen love over convenience, sacrifice over comfort.

But reality had shattered those dreams with the cruelty of a sledgehammer. The cameras were here, the microphones were ready, but the story they wanted to tell was very different. Instead of a hero, they saw a predator. Instead of inspiration, they offered condemnation. Instead of celebrating his care for a vulnerable child, they questioned his motives, suggested darkness where there had been only light.

The first reporter, a young woman with perfectly styled hair and ambitious eyes, had already prepared her questions. He couldn't hear them from behind the glass, but he could read her lips, see the practiced expression of righteous anger. She would ask about his relationship with students, about his history with children, about his fitness to be around the vulnerable. Every question would be a trap, every answer would be twisted to fit the narrative they had already written.

The dream faded completely as he watched her rehearse her opening statement, gesturing toward his building with the kind of dramatic flair that played well on television. The media had come, just as he had once imagined, but they had come to destroy rather than celebrate.

He closed the curtains and turned away from the window, away from the spectacle outside, away from the death of his dreams.

The Weight of Leaving

Later that morning, as Nandini prepared to take Pallavi to school, the magnitude of what was happening fully hit her. There was a strong possibility of Ajay being arrested, and if he was, she was responsible for a child who had already experienced more loss than most adults.

"Ajay, I don't want Pallavi to witness her beloved father being arrested. I'm taking her to my mother's place." Nandini said. "That's so kind of you, Nandini. You can't imagine how relieved I feel now." Ajay replied.

`She knelt beside Pallavi, who was carefully arranging her books in her school bag—a ritual Ajay had taught her to ensure nothing was forgotten.

"Pallavi, sweetheart," Nandini said gently, "today you're going to stay with your grandmama. My mother."

Pallavi looked up, confusion clouding her features. "But why? When is Daddy coming back?"

The question pierced through Nandini's carefully constructed composure. How do you explain to a six-year-old that her father has been arrested? How do you tell a child who has already been abandoned once that the man who saved her is now gone?

"He's... he's helping the police with some important work," Nandini said, the lie tasting like ash in her mouth. "It might take a few days."

Pallavi's eyes widened with worry. "Is he in trouble?"

"No, darling. He's just helping them understand some things. But while he's away, we need to stay somewhere safe."

The journey to her mother's house in Kothrud was tense. Pallavi sat quietly in the back seat of the car, clutching her stuffed rabbit—a gift from Ajay on her sixth birthday. Nandini watched the familiar streets pass by, each landmark bringing her closer to a confrontation she had been dreading.

Ms. Deshmukh lived in a neat two-bedroom apartment in a

middle-class society. She had lived alone since her husband's death three years ago, spending her days in a routine of prayers, television serials, and gossip with neighbours. She had strong opinions about everything, especially about her daughter's life choices.

When Nandini rang the doorbell, holding Pallavi's hand, she braced herself for the inevitable questions.

Her mother opened the door, her expression immediately shifting from surprise to concern to something that looked suspiciously like satisfaction. She had been reading the morning newspapers, had seen the headlines about Ajay's arrest.

"I saw the news," she said without preamble. "That husband of yours is finally showing his true colours."

"Ex-husband," Nandini corrected sharply. "And we need to talk."

Ms. Deshmukh's eyes fell on Pallavi, who was hiding behind Nandini's leg. "And this is...?"

"This is Pallavi. Ajay's daughter. She'll be staying with us for a few days."

The silence that followed was deafening. Ms. Deshmukh's face went through several expressions—surprise, confusion, calculation, and finally, disapproval.

"Inside," she said curtly. "Both of you."

The Reckoning

The apartment smelled of incense and old newspapers. Ms. Deshmukh had always been a meticulous housekeeper, and every surface gleamed with the attention of someone who had too much time and too many opinions. Family photographs lined the walls—wedding pictures, graduation ceremonies, festivals—a shrine to middle-class respectability.

Nandini settled Pallavi on the sofa with a colouring book, then followed her mother to the kitchen. The conversation that followed was one she had been preparing for since her divorce, but had hoped never to have.

"So," Ms. Deshmukh said, her voice dripping with vindication, "your wonderful ex-husband is on the way to jail for molesting children. Are you satisfied now?"

Nandini replied carefully. "He's innocent."

"Innocent?" Her mother's voice rose an octave. "The newspapers are calling him a predator. The school suspended him. The police arrested him. But you still think he's innocent?"

"I know he's innocent."

"You know?" Ms. Deshmukh laughed, but there was no humour in it. "You're the same girl who divorced him because he wasn't good enough for you. Now suddenly he's a saint?"

The words hit their mark. Nandini felt the familiar sting of her mother's criticism, the way she had always made her feel like every decision was wrong, every choice a mistake.

"I divorced him for other reasons," she said quietly.

"Yes, because I told you he was no good. Because I warned you that a man who couldn't even afford a proper wedding wouldn't be able to provide for a family. Because I said a teacher's salary was no foundation for a marriage."

"You said a lot of things."

"And I was right about all of them. Look at him now—arrested, suspended, disgraced. Is this the man you want to associate with? Is this the example you want to set for your life?"

Nandini turned to look at Pallavi, who was colouring with intense concentration, her small tongue poking out in focus. The child was completely absorbed in her artwork, creating a world of bright colours and simple shapes while the adults around her negotiated the complicated terrain of adult relationships.

Nandini said finally. "He's her father. And he's the closest thing to a good man I've ever known."

Ms. Deshmukh's expression hardened. "A good man? A good man doesn't get arrested for molesting children."

"A good man gets falsely accused because he's an easy target. Because he's too gentle to fight back, too trusting to see betrayal coming."

"You're deluding yourself."

"Am I?" Nandini's voice was rising now, years of pent-up frustration finally finding an outlet. "Or are you just happy to see him fall because it proves you were right about him not being good enough for your daughter?"

The accusation hung in the air like a challenge. Ms. Deshmukh's face flushed red, whether from anger or embarrassment, Nandini couldn't tell.

"How dare you—"

"How dare I what? Tell the truth? You never liked him because he didn't fit your idea of what a successful man should be. You wanted me to marry someone rich, someone with a big house and a fancy car. You never cared that he was kind, that he was honest, that he would have done anything for me."

"And where did that kindness get him? Where did that honesty get you?"

"It got him a daughter who loves him. It got him a reputation as a teacher who cared more about his students than his pay cheque."

"It got him arrested."

"It got him targeted by people who knew he wouldn't fight back."

Ms. Deshmukh shook her head in frustration. "You're making the same mistake again. You're choosing him over your own common sense."

"I'm choosing right over wrong. I'm choosing to stand by someone who stood by me when I was at my worst."

"He didn't stand by you. You left him."

"I left him because of you!" The words exploded out of Nandini before she could stop them. "Because you made me believe he wasn't enough, that I deserved better, that I was settling for less than I was worth."

The silence that followed was absolute. Even Pallavi looked up from her colouring, sensing the shift in the room's atmosphere.

Ms. Deshmukh's face went pale. She couldn't contain her tears. "I... I was trying to protect you."

"You were trying to control me. You wanted me to marry someone who would make you look good to the neighbours, someone who would validate your idea of success."

"I wanted you to be happy."

"Yes, but more than that, you wanted me to be secure. There's a difference."

The fight seemed to go out of Ms. Deshmukh all at once. She sank into a chair, suddenly looking every one of her sixty-eight years.

"I did what I thought was best," she said quietly.

"I know you did. But your best nearly destroyed the best thing in my life."

"And now?"

"Now I'm trying to fix it. And I need your help."

Ms. Deshmukh looked at her daughter with new eyes—seeing not the defiant girl who had married against her wishes, but a woman who had learned hard lessons about love and loyalty. The years of widowhood had softened some of her sharp edges, but not her protective instincts.

"What kind of help?"

"I need you to take care of Pallavi. And I need you to treat her with kindness. No questions about her background, no comments about her father, no judgment about the situation."

Ms. Deshmukh was quiet for a long moment, processing what Nandini told her. She had spent years believing she understood her ex-son-in-law, had built her disapproval on the foundation of his modest ambitions and gentle nature. But the picture Nandini was painting was more complex.

"What do you need me to do?"

"First, promise me you won't trouble her. No interrogations, no comments about her father's situation. She's already confused and scared."

"I promise."

"Second, don't let her watch the news. The media is going to turn this into a circus, and she doesn't need to see her father being called a monster."

"Understood."

"Third, if anyone asks you about the situation—neighbours, relatives, anyone—you tell them it's a private family matter and you don't discuss it."

Ms. Deshmukh nodded slowly. "What about you? What will you be doing?"

"I'm going to fight for him. I'm going to prove his innocence."

"How?"

"I don't know yet. But I'll find a way."

Ms. Deshmukh reached across the small kitchen table and took her daughter's hand. "I was wrong about him, wasn't I?"

"You were wrong about a lot of things. But you were right about one thing—I did deserve better. I deserved better than to be the kind of woman who would abandon a good man because he wasn't rich enough."

"Nandini..."

"I need to make this right, Ma. Not just for him, but for me.

Before Ms. Deshmukh could respond, Pallavi appeared in the doorway, her colouring book in hand.

"Nandini aunty," she said softly, "I drew a picture of our house. See?"

She held up the drawing—a simple house with a triangular roof, two windows, and a door. In front of the house were three stick figures: a tall man, a woman, and a small child holding hands.

"This is Daddy," she said, pointing to the tallest figure. "This is you, and this is me. We're all together."

Nandini felt tears prick her eyes. In the child's innocent drawing, they were a family—complete, happy, unified. It was the family she had walked away from, the family she was now fighting to restore.

"It's beautiful, sweetheart," she said, her voice thick with emotion.

Ms. Deshmukh looked at the drawing, then at her daughter's face, then at the small child who had drawn such a simple picture of such a complex situation.

"Pallavi," she said gently, "would you like to see my garden? I have some flowers that might be nice to colour."

Pallavi brightened immediately. "Yes, please!"

As the child ran toward the balcony, Ms. Deshmukh turned back to her daughter.

"I'll take care of her," she said quietly. "And I'll pray for him."

"Thank you."

Nandini looked toward the balcony where Pallavi was excitedly examining the marigolds and roses.

The Arrest

Two hours later, as Nandini was helping Pallavi settle into what would be her temporary room, her phone buzzed with a text from Vikrant: "They've filed an FIR. Arrest warrant issued. Where is he?"

Her blood ran cold. She had believed the initial police questioning would be enough to buy her more time, but now she knew that wasn't true. The machinery of justice, once set in motion, was difficult to stop.

She called Ajay immediately.

"They're coming for you," she said without preamble. "Vikrant says there's a warrant."

"I know," Ajay replied calmly. "I can see them from the window."

"What do you mean you can see them?"

"Police van. Three officers. They're talking to the media first."

Nandini felt panic rising in her chest. She warned Ajay "Listen to me. Once they arrest you, once you're in the system, it becomes much harder to prove your innocence. The narrative becomes that you're a criminal who was caught. Stay out of sight. Let them wait for you. In the meantime, I will consult legal counsel and apply for anticipatory bail immediately; this may provide time to prepare a defence."

"I understand. But running would make me look guilty." Said Ajay.

"And staying makes you look like a martyr." Nandini expressed her worry.

There was a long pause on the other end of the line. Finally, Ajay spoke: "I need to face this. For Pallavi's sake, for my own sake. I need to show her that when you're innocent, you don't run."

"She's six years old, Ajay. She won't understand the difference between courage and stupidity."

"Then I'll have to hope she understands when she's older."

Nandini could hear movement in the background—footsteps, voices, the sound of a door opening.

"They're here," Ajay said quietly.

"Ajay, I........."

"Take care of her. And thank you. For everything."

The line went dead.

Nandini stood in her mother's guest room, surrounded by the innocent drawings that Pallavi had taped to the walls—flowers and houses and stick-figure families—and felt the weight of the moment settle over her like a burial shroud. Somewhere across the city, the man she had once loved, had left, and was now fighting to save, was being taken into custody.

She thought about the media circus that would follow, about the photographers who would capture every moment of his humiliation, about the reporters who would dissect his life and find it wanting. She thought about the colleagues who would distance themselves, the friends who would avoid his calls, the system that would presume his guilt and demand that he proves his innocence.

But mostly, she thought about Pallavi, who was in the next room arranging her few possessions in a space that wasn't home, waiting for a father who might not come back.

The Machinery of Justice

At Shivajinagar Police Station, Sub-Inspector Patil was having what he privately called "one of those days." The kind of day where political pressure, media attention, and legal requirements all collided in a perfect storm of administrative nightmare.

The FIR had been filed by the victim's parents, making the arrest mandatory. The media was camped outside, making the arrest public.

But Patil had been a police officer for twenty-three years, and he had developed instincts about these things. Something about this case felt wrong—not the crime itself, but the way it was unfolding. The timing was too convenient, the accusation too perfect, the media response too coordinated.

He had seen real predators, had interrogated actual criminals who hurt children. They had a particular quality—a mixture of arrogance and defensiveness, of calculated charm and underlying menace. Ajay Sharma didn't fit the profile.

But profiles, instincts, and gut feelings didn't matter when there was an FIR, a warrant, and a media circus demanding action.

When Ajay arrived at the station, escorted by two constables, Patil was struck by his composure. Most people being arrested—even innocent ones—showed signs of panic, anger, or desperation. Ajay simply looked tired, as if he had been expecting this moment for a long time.

"Mr. Sharma," Patil said as they sat in the interrogation room, "you understand why you're here?"

"I understand the charges. I don't understand why they're being brought."

"The complainant alleges that you touched her inappropriately during a tutoring session."

"That's not true."

"Can you prove it?"

Ajay was quiet for a moment. "Can she prove it is true?"

"That's not how this works, Mr. Sharma. In cases involving minors, the burden of proof is different. The child's testimony carries significant weight."

"And if the child is lying under the influence of someone?"

"Why would a child lie about something like this?"

It was the question that haunted every false accusation case. Why would a child fabricate such a serious allegation? The answer, Patil knew, was usually more complex than people wanted to believe. Children could be coached, influenced, or simply confused about what had happened. They could misinterpret innocent contact or be pressured to see malice where none existed.

But explaining that to a judge, a jury, or the public was nearly impossible. The presumption of innocence was a legal principle, but in practice, accusations involving children carried a presumption of guilt that was difficult to overcome.

"I don't know why she's thinking like this," Ajay said finally. "But I know she is."

"The school has suspended you. Your colleagues have distanced themselves. The media is calling you a predator. If you're innocent, why isn't anyone standing up for you?"

"Because people are afraid. Because it's easier to believe the worst than to risk being wrong."

"And your ex-wife? She's standing by you."

"She knows me."

"She divorced you."

"She had her reasons. But she knows I would never hurt a child."

Patil leaned back in his chair, studying the man across from him. There was something almost tragic about Ajay's situation—not just the accusations, but the isolation, the way his life had been reduced to this moment in this room.

"Mr. Sharma, I'm going to ask you directly: Did you touch this child inappropriately?"

"No."

"Did you ever touch her in any way that could be misinterpreted?"

"I may have helped her with her hair once when it was caught in her backpack zipper. I may have patted her shoulder when she did well on a test. But nothing inappropriate. Nothing that any teacher wouldn't do."

"And yet she's made this allegation."

"And yet she has."

Patil made some notes in his file, then looked up again. "We'll need to process you now. Fingerprints, photographs, formal charges. You'll be held overnight pending your court appearance tomorrow."

"I understand."

"Mr. Sharma?"

"Yes?"

"I hope you're telling the truth."

"So do I, Inspector. So do I."

The Night Before

As Ajay was led to the holding cell, his mind wandered to the conversation he'd had with Pallavi the night before. She had been having trouble sleeping, worried about a math test the next day.

"Daddy," she had said, curled up next to him on the sofa, "what if I fail?"

"You won't fail," he had replied, stroking her hair. "You've been practicing, and you understand the concepts. But even if you fail, what will happen?"

"I'd have to take the test again?"

"That's right. And what would I do?"

"Help me study more?"

"Exactly. Failing isn't the end of the world, beta. It's just information—it tells us what we need to work on."

"But what if everyone laughs at me?"

"Then they're not your real friends. Real friends help each other learn and grow."

She had been quiet for a moment, then asked: "Daddy, do you ever fail at things?"

"Every day. I fail at being patient sometimes. I fail at explaining things clearly. I fail at making enough money to buy you all the things you want."

"But you never fail at being my Daddy."

The memory brought tears to his eyes now. In the holding cell, surrounded by the smell of disinfectant and despair, he wondered if he had just failed at the most important thing of all—being her father.

Outside the police station, the media was setting up for the long haul. Tomorrow's court appearance would be the main event, but tonight they would take turns maintaining the vigil, ensuring that every development was captured, every angle explored.

Inside the station, Patil was writing his report, trying to find the right words to describe a case that felt wrong from every angle. He had arrested the man, followed the procedure, done his job. But he couldn't shake the feeling that justice was not being served.

And across the city, in a small guest room in Kothrud, a six-year-old girl was falling asleep clutching a drawing of a house with three people holding hands, waiting for her father to come home.

The fire had spread, consuming everything in its path. But in the ashes, something else was beginning to grow—the seeds of truth, planted by those who refused to let an innocent man burn.

Tomorrow would bring new challenges, new revelations, new tests of character and conviction. But tonight, in the darkness of the holding cell, Ajay Sharma held onto the one thing that no false accusation could take away: the love of a child who knew, without doubt, that her father was a good man.

Chapter 5: Echoes in Courtroom

The Arena of Truth

The courtroom was packed—its benches filled with journalists, curious citizens, legal interns, and parents holding their breath. Every pair of eyes was glued to the man sitting in the dock—Ajay Sharma—once revered as the most beloved teacher in the city, now accused of an unthinkable crime.

On one side, sat the prosecution, armed with documents, testimonies, and fear. On the other side, the defence, holding stories, character, and hope.

Ajay sat between his lawyer Vikrant Shelar and his former wife Nandini, who had chosen to attend not as an ex-spouse, but as a guardian of truth. His face was calm, but his eyes were burdened with storms.

At exactly 10 AM, Judge Rajendra Kulkarni entered. The chatter died instantly.

"All rise," the bailiff announced.

Everyone stood. The solemnity of justice filled the air.

Vikrant whispered: "Today, Ajay, the weight begins to shift. Trust the truth."

Across the aisle, Prosecutor Meena Raut stood poised like a fencer, ready to strike with sharp logic and pressure.

Prosecution Witnesses

Smita Kulkarni – Mother of the Alleged Victim

Meena stepped forward with practiced confidence. "What did your daughter say when she came home?"

Smita's voice trembled slightly as she responded. "She was withdrawn. She said her teacher picked her up and patted her head. She looked scared."

"Did she use the term 'bad touch'?" Meena pressed.

"No, but... we've been teaching her about these things. And she was scared."

Vikrant rose for cross-examination, his voice gentle but probing.

"Did she say she felt unsafe?"

Smita hesitated. "No."

"So, it was your interpretation, not her words?"

"Yes. It was based on fear. Mother's instinct."

Raghav Kulkarni – Father of the alleged victim

"What was your reaction?" Meena asked.

"I was shocked. I trusted my wife's judgment. We couldn't afford to ignore it."

Vikrant's cross-examination was direct. "Did you speak to Ajay Sharma before filing a complaint?"

"No."

"Did your daughter accuse him explicitly?"

"No."

"So, this entire action is built on inference and silence?"

Raghav's admission was quiet but clear. "Yes."

Shikha Bendre – Parent of Another Student

"Have you seen Mr. Sharma interacting with children?" Meena asked.

"Yes, he was too physical. Patting, holding hands…"

Vikrant's cross-examination revealed the weakness in her testimony. "Did your daughter ever express discomfort?"

"No."

"Did you raise concerns before this case emerged in media?"

Shikha's voice was barely audible. "No."

"So, your concern came after media narratives began?"

"Yes."

Nalini Patkar – Co-Teacher and Ajay's colleague

"What did you observe?" Meena inquired.

"He was emotional. Sometimes too affectionate."

"Did you ever confront him?"

"Yes. He apologized and gave space."

Vikrant seized on this admission. "Did he ever act inappropriately in front of you?"

"No."

"Then your concern was about optics, not offense?"

"Yes."

Sub-Inspector Patil – Investigating Officer

"What did the inquiry reveal?" Meena asked.

"No physical evidence. The child was not medically distressed. Only verbal statement by parents."

"Did Mr. Sharma cooperate?"

"Fully."

Vikrant's questioning exposed the procedural nature of the arrest. "So, the arrest was precautionary?"

"Yes. No direct evidence. Just complaint pressure."

Defence Witnesses

Priya Raut – Co-teacher and Ajay's colleague

"How did Mr. Sharma behave in school?" Vikrant asked.

"He was an island of calm. Respected everyone. A gentle mentor."

Meena's cross-examination was brief. "Didn't staff whisper about his closeness with students?"

"Yes. But no one ever filed a complaint. There was nothing beyond care."

Dr. Keshav Mehra – Child Psychologist

"You met the child?" Vikrant inquired.

"Yes. She seemed confused, not traumatized."

"Your professional opinion?"

"No abuse. Just an overwhelmed child trying to process adult concepts."

Meenal Pawar – UPSC Ranker, Former Mentee

"What did Ajay Sharma mean to you?" Vikrant asked.

"He gave me books when I had none. He saw a future in me when no one else did."

"Ever felt unsafe around him?"

"Never."

Meena's question was direct. "Would you report him if you saw anything wrong?"

"Without hesitation. But I never had to."

The Six Daughters-

Vikrant addressed the judge directly. "Your Honour, these six young women represent what society often forgets—that trust and mentorship can rewrite destiny."

Aditi Sharma – Rescued Child, Now Project Head

The courtroom stirred as a confident woman in her mid-twenties walked to the witness stand. Aditi Sharma, now a successful project head at a major NGO, carried herself with the poise of someone who had travelled far from her origins.

"Please state your name and occupation for the record," Vikrant began.

"My name is Aditi Sharma. I am the Project Head for Child Rehabilitation at Asha Foundation. I hold a Master's degree in Social Work from Tata Institute of Social Sciences."

"How do you know the accused, Mr. Ajay Sharma?"

"He saved my life some 20 years ago. But more than that, he gave me a life worth living."

"Will you tell the court about your encounter with Mr. Sharma in detail?"

Aditi took a deep breath, her eyes distant as she travelled back in time.

"Your Honour, "I was six or seven- I don't remember exactly- when my parents died in a building collapse in Dharavi. I had no relatives, no one to claim me. The authorities were supposed to place me in a government home, but I never reached there. Instead, I was picked up by a man named Raju Bhai and his gang from the transit shelter itself."

The courtroom was silent, hanging on every word.

"Raju Bhai ran a begging racket in Mumbai. He had about

twenty children under his control, all of us stolen from different places - some orphaned like me, others kidnapped from railway stations, bus stops. We were his daily wage earners."

"Did you ever try to escape?"

"Once. A few days back when Ajay rescued me. I ran away but had nowhere to go. Raju Bhai found me within two days. He made an example of me - he beat me in front of all the other children and locked me in a dark room for a day without food. After that, no one dared to try again."

"Now tell the court about the day you met Mr. Ajay Sharma."

“I was at my usual spot near Dadar station. I had been coughing up blood for three days, and I was getting weaker. People were ignoring me more than usual - maybe because I looked too sick to be pitiful."

"What happened then?"

"I was sitting on the pavement, barely conscious, when I heard footsteps stop in front of me. I looked up and saw a student in uniform, Mr. Ajay. He was carrying a bag of groceries. Instead of walking past like everyone else, he knelt down beside me."

"What did he say?"

“He just looked at me with........ kind eyes. Then he asked very gently, 'Beta, when did you last eat?' His voice was so soft, so different from what I was used to hearing. I was too weak to lie, so I just shook my head."

"What did Mr. Sharma do next?"

"He opened his grocery bag and took out a banana. He peeled it and handed it to me. I was so hungry that I ate it too quickly and nearly choked. He patted my back gently and gave me water from his bottle. Then he sat down beside me on the dirty pavement, in his clean clothes, and waited for me to finish eating."

"Did he ask you questions?"

"Not immediately. He just sat with me. After I finished eating, he asked where I lived. I was trained to lie, so I said I lived with my uncle nearby. But he looked at me and said, Beta, I've been watching you for the past week sitting here and begging. No uncle would let his child do this."

"He had been observing you?"

"Yes. He told me later that he had noticed me during his daily commute to college. He had seen me getting thinner each day, coughing more, and he couldn't ignore it anymore."

"What happened next?"

"He asked me if I wanted to go to a doctor. I was terrified because Raju Bhai had told us never to go with strangers. But I was so sick, and this man seemed different. He waited for my answer."

"What did you decide?"

"I said yes. He helped me stand up - I was so weak I could barely walk. He supported me gently and took me to a nearby clinic. The doctor examined me and said I had severe malnutrition and a chest infection. Ajay Sir got medicines for me. He was giving me the medicines and some food twice a day while on the way to his college and back home."

"Did he ask you to come with him?"

"No. He said, 'Beta, I don't know what your situation is, but if you ever need help, I'll be here at this same time tomorrow.' He gave me his handkerchief and 50 rupees and left."

"Did you meet him the next day?"

"Yes. When I went back to my shelter in the evening, I was beaten by Raju Bhai for earning less money - Ajay Sir saw the fresh bruises when he came. He didn't say anything, just gave me food again."

"How long did this continue?"

"For two weeks. Every day, he would come, give me food and just sit with me. He never asked invasive questions. He never made me feel ashamed. He just showed up, consistently, like a ray of light in my darkness."

"When did you tell him the truth?"

"After two weeks. I was very sick again, and I was terrified that if I died, no one would even know my real name. So, I told him everything - about Raju Bhai, about the other children, about the warehouse, about the beatings."

"What was his reaction?"

“He just listened. When I finished, he said, 'Beta, you're going to be safe now. But I need you to trust me and be very brave.' He explained that he would bring help to rescue not just me, but all the children."

"How did the rescue happen?"

"Ajay Sir had contacted an NGO and the police. Three days later, when we were all in the warehouse, there was a sudden commotion. The police broke down the door. Raju Bhai and his men were arrested. We were all freed."

"What happened to you after the rescue?"

"We were taken to a government shelter. Ajay worked with the NGO to ensure we were properly rehabilitated. He visited us regularly, brought us books, toys, and most importantly, hope."

"Did he place you in a permanent home?"

"Yes. He found a children's home run by Sister Margaret in Bandra. But it wasn't just placement - he ensured the place was good, that we would be treated well, educated properly. He personally vouched for our care."

"Did his involvement end there?"

"No. He continued to visit us every week for years. He brought us study materials, helped with our homework, encouraged us to dream beyond our circumstances. He arranged for proper teachers to come to the children's home. He made sure we all learned to read and write."

"What was his approach toward you children?"

"By age, he was like an elder brother to us, but in terms of his role in our growth, he was a father figure. He always respected our boundaries. When he patted our heads or hugged us, it felt safe — protective."

"Did he ever show favouritism?"

"No. He treated all of us equally. Whether we were quick learners or slow, whether we were obedient or rebellious, he showed the same patience and care to everyone."

"How did you progress academically?"

"Under his guidance, I completed my schooling. He encouraged me to aim higher. When I expressed interest in social work, he helped me understand the field, arranged for me to meet professionals, and supported my college applications."

"Did he support you financially?"

"He contributed to our education, but he also taught us the value of hard work. He arranged part-time jobs for us when we were old enough, not just to earn money, but to build our confidence and skills."

"How many children were rescued in total?"

"Seventeen children were rescued from Raju Bhai's racket. Out of these, twelve were successfully rehabilitated and went on to lead productive lives. Five were reunited with their families."

"What happened to the other children who were with you?"

"All of them are doing well today. Priya became a nurse, Suresh is an auto-rickshaw driver with his own vehicle, Meera works in a bank. We stay in touch, and we all remember who gave us these opportunities."

"How has this experience shaped your career?"

"It made me realize that one person's intervention can change multiple lives. That's why I chose to work in child rehabilitation. I wanted to be for other children what Ajay Sir was for me."

"In all your years of knowing Mr. Sharma, did you ever witness or experience any inappropriate behaviour?"

"Never. Not once. He was always proper, always respectful. He taught us about good touch and bad touch. He made us aware of our rights. He protected us from harm, he never caused it."

"What is your professional opinion about the allegations against Mr. Sharma?"

Meena stood quickly. "Objection, Your Honour. The witness is not qualified to give expert testimony on this matter."

Judge Kulkarni nodded. "Sustained. The witness may speak from personal experience only."

Vikrant adjusted his approach. "Based on your personal experience with Mr. Sharma over nearly two decades, what is your assessment of his character?"

"He is a man who sees children as human beings deserving of dignity and respect. He is incapable of harming a child. The man who saved so many children from a life of misery and exploitation could never be the man described in these charges."

"No further questions, Your Honour."

Cross-Examination by Prosecutor Meena Raut

Meena approached the witness stand with calculated precision. "Ms. Sharma, you've painted a very touching picture of Mr. Ajay Sharma. But isn't it true that your gratitude toward him might cloud your judgment?"

"My gratitude is based on facts, not fantasy. I've had twenty years to analyse his actions objectively."

"You said he watched you for one week before approaching. Isn't that stalking behaviour?"

"No, it's an observation born of concern. If he had ill intentions, he would have approached me when I was alone and vulnerable, not taken me to a doctor and involved other adults."

"But you were a child then. How can you be certain of his intentions?"

"Because his actions were consistent over decades. He never isolated any of us. He never asked us to keep secrets. He never tried to separate us from our caregivers. These are classic signs of grooming, and none of them were present."

"You say he never touched you inappropriately. But as a child, would you have recognized inappropriate touch?"

"He himself taught us about appropriate and inappropriate touch. He explained the difference clearly. He told us that no one, including him, should ever touch us in ways that made us uncomfortable."

"Isn't it convenient that he taught you these concepts? Couldn't that be a way to normalize his behaviour?"

"No. He taught us to be vigilant about everyone, including figures of authority. He never put himself above suspicion. He encouraged us to report any uncomfortable situation to Sister Margaret or the NGO workers."

"You've built your entire career on child welfare. Wouldn't exposing Mr. Sharma as an abuser damage your professional reputation?"

"My reputation would be damaged if I protected an abuser, not if I exposed one. But I'm not protecting him - I'm stating facts based on my experience."

"How do you know what happened to other children when you weren't present?"

"We lived together, shared our experiences. Children talk to each other. If any of us had been uncomfortable with Ajay Sir, we would have known."

"But children also keep secrets, especially when they're afraid or confused."

"True. But fear and confusion create behavioural changes. None of us showed signs of trauma or distress after spending time with Ajay Sir. In fact, we all showed improvement."

"You said he visited you weekly for years. Isn't that excessive involvement?"

"It's commitment. He didn't just rescue us and forget about us. He ensured our long-term welfare. That's the difference between a saviour and an opportunist."

"Could his continued involvement have created an unhealthy dependency?"

"No. He gradually reduced his involvement as we became more independent. He taught us to stand on our own feet, not to depend on him forever."

"You call yourself Aditi Sharma, you've adopted his family name. Doesn't that suggest an emotional dependency?"

"I adopted his family name because he gave me an identity

when I had none. It's not romantic attachment - it's the acknowledgment of a father figure. Many adopted children take their guardian's surname."

"But he never formally adopted you, did he?"

"No, but he performed the role of a father. Legal adoption wasn't a question. When he rescued me, he was hardly in his early twenties, and we were seventeen children. He provided care and guidance to all of us."

"Ms. Sharma, you've testified that Mr. Ajay Sharma is incapable of harming a child. But people can behave differently in different situations with different children, can't they?"

"That's a theoretical possibility, but it's not consistent with everything I know about him. A person's character is revealed through their actions over time, not through isolated incidents."

"Have you met the child who has made these allegations?"

"No, I have not."

"Then how can you be certain about what happened in this specific case?"

"I can't speak to the specific incident, but I can speak to the character of the man accused. The person I know could not have committed this act."

"But you acknowledge that you can't know everything about a person, can you?"

"I acknowledge that I can't know everything. But I can know enough to form a judgment based on years of observation and interaction."

"No further questions, Your Honour."

Re-examination by Defence

Vikrant rose for re-examination. "Ms. Sharma, the prosecutor suggested that Mr. Ajay Sharma might behave differently with different children. In your experience, did you observe him interacting with children other than your group?"

"Yes. He interacted with children at various schools, at the children's home, and in the community. His behaviour was consistent - always respectful, always appropriate."

"Did you ever see him alone with a child?"

"Yes, but always in appropriate settings - tutoring sessions in open spaces, counselling sessions with doors open, or public places. He never sought isolation with children."

"In your professional capacity, have you encountered cases of child abuse?"

"Yes, unfortunately, many."

"Based on that experience, do you see any patterns in Mr. Sharma's behaviour that resemble those of abusers?"

"No. Abusers typically isolate their victims, create dependency, demand secrecy, and gradually escalate their behaviour. Mr. Sharma did none of these things."

"Thank you. No further questions."

The courtroom was silent as Aditi stepped down from the witness stand. Her testimony had been powerful, detailed, and unwavering. She had painted a picture of a man who had dedicated his life to protecting children, not harming them.

As she walked back to her seat, she looked at Ajay Sharma. Their eyes met for a moment, and she saw the same kindness that had saved her life twenty years ago. In that moment, she silently promised him that she would continue to fight for the truth, just as he had fought for her life all those years ago.

The courtroom remained hushed, the weight of her words

hanging in the air like a prayer for justice.

Asha Sharma – Mobile Library Organizer

The next witness was a woman in her late twenties, wearing a simple saree with an air of quiet dignity. As she walked to the witness stand, her confident stride told a story of transformation.

"Please state your name and occupation," Vikrant began.

"My name is Asha. I run a mobile library service for rural children in Maharashtra. I am also pursuing my PhD in Library Sciences from Pune University."

"How did you meet Mr. Ajay Sharma?"

"I was six years old when I first encountered him. But that encounter was preceded by two years of hell."

"Your Honour, I need to take the court back in my past. I was four years old, living with my grandmother in a small village near Nashik. I had lost my parents in a road accident. She was very old and sick. One day, she didn't wake up. I was alone, scared, and hungry."

"What happened next?" Vikrant asked.

"Some neighbours took me to the district collector's office. I was supposed to be sent to a government facility, but during the transfer, I was... taken. A man named Bhola convinced the escort that he was my relative and would take care of me."

"But he wasn't your relative?"

"No. He was a trafficker who sold children to begging rings. He sold me to a woman named Kamala who ran a begging operation near Pune railway station."

"Did you ever try to escape?"

"Where would I go? I was four, then five, then six. I didn't even remember my real name. I only knew that platform, those people, and the constant fear of not earning enough."

"Tell the court about the day you met Mr. Sharma."

"It was a monsoon. I was six years old. I was standing outside the railway station, completely soaked, shivering. Most passengers were running to avoid the rain, so I wasn't earning anything."

"What happened then?"

"A boy hardly 14 or 15, emerged from the station, saw me standing there, and stopped. Instead of walking away like everyone else, he approached me. He asked, 'What is your name, where is your mother?' I was trained to say she was sick and needed money for medicine."

"What did Mr. Sharma do?"

" He looked around, saw that I was alone, and asked, 'Where do you live?' I pointed vaguely toward the platform. He said, 'Show me.' I was scared because Kamala had told us never to bring strangers to our sleeping place."

"Did you take him there?"

"I had no choice. He was insistent but gentle. When we reached the platform, he saw the other children, the dirty rags we slept on, and he immediately understood what was happening."

"What was his reaction?"

"He didn't get angry or create a scene. He sat down with us, asked our names, and started talking to us like we were normal children, not beggars. He bought us food and asked who was looking after us."

"Did you tell him about Kamala?"

"The other children were too scared, but I was so hungry and tired that I told him everything. He listened without interrupting. Then he said, You don't have to live like this anymore."

"What did he do next?"

"He stayed with us for some time. He bought us more food, He told us he would come back the next day and asked us to wait for him."

"Did he return?"

"Yes. He came back with a woman from an NGO and two policemen. When Kamala saw them, she tried to run, but they caught her. She was arrested, and we were rescued."

"What happened to you after the rescue?"

"We were taken to a children's home in Pune. Mr. Sharma didn't just drop us off - he ensured we were properly admitted, that we had medical check-ups, and that we were given proper clothes, food and education."

"Did his involvement end there?"

"No. He visited us almost every two weeks. He brought us books, toys, and most importantly, he helped us remember who we were. He worked with the social workers to trace our backgrounds."

"Were you able to reconnect with your family?"

"My grandmother was dead, and I had no other family. But Mr. Sharma made sure I felt like I belonged somewhere. He helped me choose the name 'Asha' - it means hope."

"How did he help with your education?"

"He enrolled me in a proper school. When I struggled with studies because I had never been to school before, he arranged for extra tutoring. He came himself sometimes to help with my homework."

"Did he ever behave inappropriately with you?"

"Never. He was always respectful. When he patted my head or congratulated me for good grades, it felt like what I imagined a father's touch would feel like - safe and encouraging."

"How did you develop your interest in library work?"

"Mr. Sharma introduced me to books. He showed me that stories could take me to different worlds. He said that every child deserved access to books, regardless of where they lived. That's how I decided to create mobile libraries for rural children."

"In all your years of knowing him, did you ever feel unsafe?"

"Never. He taught me to distinguish between safe and unsafe touch. He made me aware of my rights. He protected me from harm - he never caused it."

“Your Honour, I have no further questions for this witness. Ms. Meena, you may proceed with your cross-examination.

Cross-Examination by Prosecutor

Meena approached with her characteristic directness. "Ms. Asha, you were very young when you met Mr. Sharma. Could your memories be idealized?"

"I have thought about this many times. But some experiences are too profound to forget or misremember. Being rescued from hell is one such experience."

"You said he visited you regularly. Didn't you find it strange that an adult man was so interested in children?"

"He wasn't the only adult involved. There were NGO workers, social workers, teachers. His visits were always transparent and purposeful."

"But you've named yourself after him - Asha Sharma. Isn't that an unhealthy attachment?"

"Ajay chose the name Asha for me, it means hope. I added Sharma because he gave me that hope. It's gratitude, not attachment."

"How do you know he didn't behave differently with other children?"

"Because I lived with other children he had helped. We shared our experiences. None of us ever felt uncomfortable or unsafe with him."

"No further questions."

Bhavna Desai – Trauma Counsellor

A woman in her early thirties, wearing a formal blazer, approached the witness stand. Her professional demeanour was evident, but there was a depth in her eyes that spoke of personal experience with trauma.

"Please state your name and occupation," Vikrant requested.

"I am Bhavna Desai. I am a licensed trauma counsellor specializing in child abuse cases. I work with the State Child Protection Unit."

"How did you meet Mr. Ajay Sharma?"

"I was eight years old when he saved me from what could have been the worst night of my life."

"Your Honour, I need to take the court back to a dark alley in Dadar in 1992. I was walking home from my evening tuition class when three older boys cornered me."

"They were trying to drag me into a narrow lane. I was screaming, but the area was isolated, and no one was coming to help. I thought... I thought that was the end of my childhood."

"How did Mr. Sharma come into the picture?"

"He was returning from his college, carrying some books. He heard my screams and came running. He didn't hesitate for a second. He picked up a wooden stick from the ground and charged at those boys and chased them away. They were young and aggressive - but he didn't think about his own safety. He just protected me."

"What happened after the boys fled?"

"I was in shock, crying uncontrollably. Mr. Sharma spoke to me in a calm, soothing voice. He asked if I was hurt, if I knew my parents' phone number."

"Did he take you home?"

"First, he insisted we go to the police station to file a report. Even though I was scared and just wanted to go home, he explained that reporting was important so those boys wouldn't hurt other children."

"He made sure the police took my statement properly, that they understood the seriousness of the situation. He stayed with me throughout the process."

"Did he take you home after that?"

"Yes, but he didn't go alone. He asked a female constable to accompany us. He explained to my parents what had happened, and he made sure they understood that I had done nothing wrong."

"Did your interaction with Mr. Sharma continue after that incident?"

"Yes. He checked on me regularly to make sure I was recovering emotionally. He arranged for me to speak with a counsellor because he was concerned about the psychological impact of the incident."

"How did he help you process the trauma?"

"He helped me understand that it wasn't my fault. He made me feel empowered rather than victimized."

"Did you ever feel uncomfortable with his attention?"

"Never. His concern was always appropriate and professional. He involved my parents in everything."

"How did this experience influence your career choice?"

"Seeing how Mr. Sharma handled my trauma - with sensitivity, professionalism, and genuine care - inspired me to help other children who had experienced similar situations. I wanted to provide the same kind of support he had given me."

"In your personal capacity, how do you view Mr. Sharma's behaviour?"

"As a trauma counsellor, I can say that his approach was textbook perfect. He protected me, empowered me, involved appropriate authorities, and ensured proper follow-up care. This is exactly how such situations should be handled."

"Based on your professional experience, do you see any signs of predatory behaviour in Mr. Sharma's actions?"

"Absolutely not. Predators isolate their victims, create dependency, and gradually normalize inappropriate behaviour. Mr. Sharma did the opposite - he empowered me, involved other adults, and maintained appropriate boundaries."

Cross-Examination by Prosecutor

Meena stepped forward. "Ms. Desai, you were traumatized when you met Mr. Sharma. Could your gratitude be colouring your perception?"

"I've considered that possibility. But my professional training has taught me to analyse situations objectively. Even viewing that incident through my professional lens, his behaviour was exemplary."

"You said he arranged counselling for you. Isn't it unusual for a college boy to take such personal interest in a girl's mental health?"

"It shows extraordinary dedication to child welfare. Many adults would have considered their job done after the immediate rescue. He went above and beyond."

"But couldn't such involvement be a way to gain access to vulnerable children?"

"If that were his intention, he would have tried to become my counsellor himself. Instead, he connected me with a professional and maintained appropriate boundaries."

"As a trauma counsellor, you must know that predators can be very skilled at manipulation."

"Yes, and I also know the signs to look for. Mr. Sharma exhibited none of them. His actions were transparent, involved multiple adults, and focused on my empowerment, not his gratification."

"No further questions."

Chitra Joshi– Anti-Trafficking Investigator

A stern-looking woman in her early thirties stepped forward. Her bearing suggested someone accustomed to confronting difficult truths and dangerous situations.

"Please state your name and occupation," Vikrant began.

"I am Chitra Joshi. I am an investigator with the Anti-Human Trafficking Unit of Mumbai Police. I have been working in this field for eight years."

"How did you meet Mr. Ajay Sharma?"

"He rescued me from a trafficking ring when I was seven years old."

"Your Honour, I was born in a small village in Uttar Pradesh. When I was six, my parents died in a flood. I was taken to an orphanage, but I was kidnapped from there by traffickers."

"What happened to you?" Vikrant asked.

"I was brought to Mumbai and sold to a man who ran a begging and petty crime ring. Children were kept in a locked room during the day and forced to work at night."

"What kind of work?"

"Pickpocketing, begging, and sometimes we were rented out to other criminals for various illegal activities. We lived in constant fear."

"How did Mr. Sharma find you?"

"One night, I was trying to steal food from a garbage bin behind a restaurant. I was caught by the restaurant owner who started beating me. Mr. Sharma was having dinner there and heard the commotion."

"What did he do?"

"He came out and stopped the man from hitting me. Instead of calling the police on me, he bought me food and sat with me while I ate. He asked me about my situation."

"Did you tell him the truth?"

"I was too scared initially. But he was patient. He didn't pressure me. He just kept providing food and slowly gained my trust. After a week of these encounters, I told him everything."

"What was his response?"

"He was angry, but not at me. He was angry at the people who were exploiting children. He promised to help me, but he also warned me that it might be dangerous and asked if I was ready to be brave."

"How did the rescue happen?"

"Mr. Sharma worked with the police and an NGO. He helped plan the raid on the place where we were kept. When the police broke in, he was there too, calling out our names, making sure we were all found."

"What happened after the rescue?"

"We were placed in a rehabilitation centre. Mr. Sharma visited regularly, brought us books and toys, and helped us adjust to normal life. He also ensured we received counselling to deal with our trauma."

"How did he help with your education?"

"He recognized that I was intelligent and encouraged me to study. He helped me get admission to a good school and supported my education throughout. He often said that education was the best protection against exploitation."

"Did you ever feel uncomfortable with his attention?"

"Never. He was always professional and appropriate. He taught us about personal safety and encouraged us to report any uncomfortable situations to the authorities."

"How did this experience influence your career choice?"

"I chose to work in anti-trafficking because I wanted to help other children like me. I wanted to be part of the solution. Mr. Sharma's example showed me that one person can make a difference."

"In your personal capacity, how do you view Mr. Sharma's approach to child protection?"

"His approach was exemplary. He understood the complexities of trafficking, worked with appropriate authorities, and focused on long-term rehabilitation rather than just immediate rescue."

"Based on your professional experience, do you see any signs of predatory behaviour in Mr. Sharma?"

"Absolutely not. Predators exploit vulnerability for their own gain. Mr. Sharma consistently worked to eliminate vulnerability and empower children.

Cross-Examination by Prosecutor

"Ms. Joshi, you work in law enforcement. You must understand that criminals can be very sophisticated in their methods," Meena stated.

"Yes, and I also understand that consistent patterns of behaviour over decades are difficult to fake. Mr. Sharma's pattern has always been protection, not exploitation."

"But you were young when you met him. Could you have misunderstood his intentions?"

"I was young, but I had already experienced exploitation. I knew the difference between someone who wanted to help and someone who wanted to use me. Mr. Sharma was clearly in the first category."

"As a law enforcement officer, if you had evidence of his guilt, would you pursue it?"

"Without hesitation. My job is to protect children, regardless of my personal feelings. But I have no such evidence because there is none."

"No further questions."

Devika Mehta– Legal Aid Advocate

A composed woman in her early thirties, wearing lawyer's robes, approached the witness stand. Her professional attire and confident bearing suggested someone well-versed in legal proceedings.

"Please state your name and occupation," Vikrant requested.

"I am Devika Mehta. I am a legal aid advocate specializing in child rights and family law. I work with the Legal Services Authority."

"How did you meet Mr. Ajay Sharma?"

"He saved my life when I was ten years old, and then he gave me a new identity and purpose."

"Your Honour, I need to take the court back to one of the darkest chapters in recent Mumbai history - the Andheri family suicide case.

"Can you elaborate?" Vikrant asked.

"My father was a small businessman who had taken loans from multiple sources. When his business failed, he couldn't repay the debts. The moneylenders were threatening us daily. My father fell into deep depression."

"What happened then?"

"One night, my father decided to end it all. He mixed rat poison in our dinner. My parents and my younger brother died that night. I survived because I had eaten very little - I wasn't feeling well."

"How did Mr. Sharma come into your life?"

"I was hospitalized for weeks. I had no relatives, no one to claim me. Mr. Sharma read about our case in the newspaper and came to the hospital to see me."

"What did he do?"

"He didn't just visit once and leave. He came every day for two months while I was recovering. He brought books, helped me with my studies, and most importantly, he talked to me about having a future."

"How did he help you emotionally?"

"I was devastated, guilty, and angry. I felt like I should have died with my family. Mr. Sharma helped me understand that surviving meant I had a purpose to fulfil. He helped me see that I could Honour my family's memory by living meaningfully."

"What happened when you were discharged from the hospital?"

"Mr. Sharma had arranged for me to stay at a children's home. But he didn't just drop me off. He ensured that the facility was good, that I would receive proper care and education."

"Did he continue to support you?"

"Yes, throughout my schooling and college. He helped me choose the name 'Devika' - it means 'little goddess' - because he said I was blessed to have survived for a purpose."

"How did you develop your interest in law?"

"Mr. Sharma introduced me to the concept of justice. He explained that what happened to my family was not just a personal tragedy but a systemic failure. He encouraged me to study law so I could help other families facing similar situations."

"Did he support your legal education?"

"He helped me get scholarships and provided moral support throughout my studies. He attended my graduation and was prouder than any parent could be."

"In all your years of knowing him, did you ever feel uncomfortable or unsafe?"

"Never. He was always respectful, always appropriate. He taught me to understand my rights and to stand up for myself. He empowered me rather than making me dependent."

"As a legal advocate, how do you view the current allegations against Mr. Sharma?"

"From a legal perspective, these allegations are based on speculation and fear rather than evidence. The pattern of Mr. Sharma's behaviour over decades contradicts the allegations completely."

Cross-Examination by Prosecutor

"Ms. Mehta, you've built your career on Mr. Sharma's support. Doesn't that create a conflict of interest in your testimony?" Meena asked.

"My career is built on my own hard work and dedication. Mr. Sharma provided initial support, but I earned my achievements. And as a legal professional, I understand the importance of objective testimony."

"But you've taken his surname. Isn't that an indication of unhealthy attachment?"

"I took the name he gave me because it represented my rebirth. It's a professional name I use in court. It's not romantic attachment - it's professional identity."

"As a legal advocate, you must know that character witnesses can be deceived."

"I also know that consistent patterns of behaviour over decades are reliable indicators of character. Mr. Sharma's pattern has always been protection and empowerment of children."

"Could your traumatic experience have affected your judgment about Mr. Sharma?"

"My traumatic experience taught me to recognize genuine care from exploitation. Mr. Sharma's care was genuine, transparent, and focused on my wellbeing rather than his needs."

"No further questions."

Fatima Ali– National Award-Winning Poet

The final witness was a young woman in her late twenties, wearing a simple salwar kameez with a dupatta. She carried herself with quiet dignity and spoke in a clear, measured voice.

"Please state your name and occupation," Vikrant began.

"I am Fatima Ali. I am a poet and writer. I have received the National Award for Literature for my work on women's rights and social justice."

"How did you meet Mr. Ajay Sharma?"

"He saved me from a forced marriage when I was twelve years old."

"Your Honour, I come from a conservative family in the slums of Bandra. My father died when I was ten, and my mother struggled to make ends meet. My uncle convinced her that marrying me off would solve our financial problems."

"What happened?" Vikrant asked.

"When I was twelve, they arranged my marriage to a man who was forty years old. I was terrified, but I had no choice. The marriage ceremony was taking place in a small hall."

"How did Mr. Sharma intervene?"

"He had heard about the marriage from someone in the community who was concerned. He came to the marriage hall with two social workers and a police officer."

"What did he do?"

"He walked straight to the mandap where the ceremony was taking place and stopped it. He told everyone that child marriage was illegal and that he would not allow it to proceed."

"What was the reaction?"

"There was chaos. My family was angry, the groom's family was threatening. But Mr. Sharma stood firm. He explained the law to everyone and warned them about the consequences of child marriage."

"What happened to you?"

"Mr. Sharma took me to a safe place and explained my rights.

He told me that I had the right to education, to choose my own future, and to marry only when I was ready and with someone I chose."

"Did your family accept this?"

"Initially, they were angry. But Mr. Sharma worked with them patiently. He helped them understand that my education would actually improve our family's financial situation in the long run."

"How did he support your education?"

"He enrolled me in school and arranged for me to stay at a hostel for girls. He provided books and other educational materials. He also encouraged my interest in writing and poetry."

"How did you develop your literary career?"

"Mr. Sharma recognized my talent for writing and encouraged me to participate in competitions. He helped me get published in local magazines and supported my higher education in literature."

"Did he ever behave inappropriately with you?"

"Never. He was always respectful and maintained appropriate boundaries. He treated me like a daughter, not as someone to be exploited."

"How has your experience with Mr. Sharma influenced your work?"

"My poetry often deals with themes of justice, protection of the vulnerable, and the power of education. Mr. Sharma's example taught me that one person can make a difference in many lives."

"As someone who writes about social issues, how do you view these allegations?"

"These allegations are tragic not just for Mr. Sharma, but for all the children who need protection. They create fear around genuine efforts to help vulnerable children."

Cross-Examination by Prosecutor

"Ms. Ali, you've built your literary career around social justice themes. Isn't supporting Mr. Sharma part of your narrative?" Meena asked.

"My support for Mr. Sharma is based on truth, not narrative. Truth is the foundation of all meaningful literature."

"But you were very young when he helped you. Could you have misunderstood his motivations?"

"I was young, but I understood the difference between exploitation and protection. Mr. Sharma offered protection without asking for anything in return."

"As a writer, you must understand that people can present different faces to the world."

"I also understand that authentic character reveals itself through consistent actions over time. Mr. Sharma's character has been consistent for decades."

"No further questions, your honour. My next witness is Ms. Nandini Sharma. Please allow me to call her to the witness box."

"Permission granted"

Nandini Sharma – Ajay's Ex-Wife (Extended Version)

Vikrant approached the witness stand with visible reverence. "Ms. Nandini, please tell the court about your marriage to the accused."

Nandini took a deep breath, her voice steady but carrying the weight of years of reflection. "Your Honour, I was married to Ajay for seven years. They were the most transformative years of my life - not because they were easy, but because they taught me what true character looks like."

Vikrant: What kind of husband was he?

"He was..." Nandini paused, searching for words that could capture the complexity of their relationship. "He was gentle in a world that mistakes gentleness for weakness. He would wake up at 5 AM to prepare lessons, not because he had to, but because he believed every child deserved his absolute best."

Her voice grew stronger. "I would find him at our kitchen table at midnight, cutting out paper stars and drawing smiley faces on them - hundreds of them - because he wanted each of his students to feel special. He spent his own salary on books for children whose parents couldn't afford them."

Vikrant: You divorced him. Can you tell us why?

The question hung heavy in the courtroom. Nandini's composure wavered slightly, tears gathering in her eyes. "We lost our daughter, Pallavi, in a tragic accident. She was six years old - the same age as many of his students."

She wiped her eyes but continued, her voice breaking. "In my grief, I blamed him. I let others convince me that his gentleness, his dedication to teaching, somehow made him... inadequate. I was drowning in loss, and instead of holding onto the one person who understood my pain, I pushed him away."

Vikrant: What was his reaction to the divorce?

"He never fought it. Even in his own devastation, he was more concerned about my healing than his own rights. He signed every paper without argument. That's who Ajay is - he puts others' wellbeing above his own, even when they're destroying him."

Vikrant: You're here today, supporting him. Why?

Nandini stood straighter, her voice ringing with conviction. "Because I spent four years learning the difference between a good man and a perfect life. Ajay isn't perfect - no one is. But he's good.

Fundamentally, unshakably good."

She looked directly at Ajay, tears streaming down her face. "When he called me that night, accused and alone, with nowhere to turn - I realized something. In all our years together, through all our struggles, he never once raised his voice at me or our daughter. Never once showed impatience with children. He would get frustrated with work, with bills- but never with children. That's not something you fake for twelve years."

Vikrant: Tell us about his relationship with his adopted daughter, Pallavi.

Nandini's face lit up through her tears. "He found her abandoned, starving, afraid of the world. Within months, she was laughing, learning, trusting again. I've watched them together - there's no performance there, no calculation. Just a father who sees his child as a miracle, and a child who sees her father as safety itself."

She paused, gathering her strength for what came next. "Your Honour, I made the worst mistake of my life when I walked away from this man. But watching him with that little girl, seeing how he's transformed not just her life but thousands of others - I understand now that I didn't leave because he was inadequate. I left because I was broken, and I couldn't see past my own pain to recognize the gift I had."

Cross-Examination by Meena:

Meena: Ms. Nandini, you divorced him once. Isn't your support now just guilt?

Nandini's response was immediate and fierce. "Guilt would have made me send money or write a letter. Love brought me to that police station at midnight. Love made me stand in this courtroom facing judgment from people who think I'm naive or seeking attention."

Meena: But you did leave him. You did think he was inadequate for four years.

"Yes, I did. And I was wrong." Nandini's voice was steady now, unashamed. "I let grief and other people's opinions cloud my judgment. I left the best man I've ever known because I was too broken to see clearly."

Meena: How do we know you're seeing clearly now?

Nandini looked around the courtroom, her gaze settling on the six women sitting behind Ajay. "Because I lived with him for seven years. I saw him concerned for children he couldn't help, spend sleepless nights worrying about students who were struggling, give away our grocery money to buy books for kids whose parents couldn't afford them."

Her voice grew stronger. "I also watched him with others who needed saving. Look at them - Aditi, Asha, Bhavna, Chitra, Devika, Fatima. Six women who were broken children when he found them. Now they're leaders, professionals, mothers, advocates. I wasn't one of the children he rescued - I was his equal, his partner, someone who chose to love him and then chose to leave him. But I've seen how he transforms the lives of those who truly need saving. You don't create that kind of transformation through manipulation or abuse. You create it through love."

Meena: Yet you still divorced him.

"Yes, and it was the greatest mistake of my life." Nandini's voice broke with raw honesty. "Not because he was perfect, but because he was good. And in a world that often mistakes kindness for weakness, goodness for naivety, service for failure - I was foolish enough to let others convince me that what he offered wasn't enough."

She looked directly at the prosecutor. "You want to know why I'm here? Because some mistakes are so profound that you spend the rest of your life trying to make amends. Because some people are so rare that losing them changes you forever. Because some truths are so important that you risk everything to speak them."

Meena: You said he spent your grocery money on books for children. Didn't that create financial strain in your marriage?

Nandini's eyes flashed with a mixture of pain and pride. "Yes, it did. There were nights we ate bread and tea because he'd bought school supplies for children who couldn't afford them. There were times I resented it, times I felt he cared more about other people's children than his own family."

Her voice softened. "But I understand now what I couldn't see then. He wasn't choosing them over us - he was showing us what unconditional love looks like. He was teaching our daughter that in this world, you measure your wealth not by what you accumulate, but by what you give away."

Meena: So you're admitting there were problems in your marriage?"

"Yes, there were problems. But they weren't his character flaws - they were my inability to understand his character strengths." Nandini's voice was clear now, certain. "I wanted him to be more ambitious, more focused on our financial security. I didn't understand then that his ambition was measured in transformed lives, not bank balances. His security came from knowing children were safe and learning, not from stock portfolios."

Re-examination by Vikrant: Ms. Nandini, in all your years with Mr. Sharma, did you ever fear for a child's safety around him?

"Never. Not once. Children gravitated toward him like flowers toward sunlight. I've seen him with sick children, angry children, frightened children - his response was always the same. Infinite patience, absolute respect for their dignity, unwavering belief in their potential."

Vikrant: Can you give us a specific example?

Nandini smiled through her tears. "When our daughter Pallavi was four, she went through a phase of terrible nightmares. Night after night, she would wake up screaming. Ajay would sit with her for hours - sometimes until dawn - never showing impatience, never raising his voice. He would tell her stories, sing lullabies, hold her until she felt safe enough to sleep again."

Her voice grew tender. "One night, I found him asleep on the floor beside her bed. He had been there all night, his hand reaching through the bed rails to hold hers, so she would know even in sleep that she wasn't alone. That's not the behaviour of someone who harms children - that's the behaviour of someone who would die before letting a child feel afraid."

Vikrant: What would you say to the parents who filed this complaint?

Nandini's voice softened with empathy. "I understand their fear. As parents, we're terrified of the monsters that exist in this world. But in our fear, we can't afford to destroy the angels. Ajay Sharma is not the danger we need to protect our children from - he's the protection our children need from real danger."

She paused, her voice growing stronger. "I lost my child to a tragic accident, and in my grief, I blamed the one person who loved her as much as I did. These parents are afraid of losing their child to harm, but they're trying to destroy the one person who would move heaven and earth to keep her safe. Don't let fear make you do what grief made me do. Don't push away the people who are actually on your side."

Vikrant: One final question, Ms. Nandini. If you could do it all over again, would you marry Ajay Sharma?"

Nandini looked directly at Ajay, her eyes shining with tears and love. "In a heartbeat. And this time, I would be worthy of him. This time, I would understand that I wasn't marrying just a man - I was marrying a mission. And that mission was the most beautiful thing I could ever be part of."

Vikrant: No further questions, Your Honour.

As Nandini stepped down from the witness stand, the courtroom was completely silent. Her testimony had been more than legal evidence - it had been a confession, an apology, and a love letter all at once. She had laid bare her own failures to illuminate his character, and in doing so, had created one of the most powerful moments of the entire trial.

Ajay's eyes followed her as she returned to her seat, and for a moment, their eyes met across the courtroom. In that glance was forgiveness, understanding, and the recognition that sometimes the greatest love stories are not about perfect people, but about broken people who find the courage to see and speak truth.

The judge made a note in his file, visibly moved by what he had witnessed. Even the prosecutor sat quietly, perhaps understanding that she had just witnessed not just testimony, but transformation.

Vikrant: Your Honour, I have one more witness who can speak to Mr. Sharma's professional contributions - someone who witnessed first-hand the transformation he brought to education.

Judge Kulkarni: Proceed.

Vikrant: I call Ms. Vandana Joshi, Ex Principal of Vidya Vihar High School.

Ms. Joshi approached the witness stand, her earlier guilt about suspending Ajay evident in her demeanour. This was her chance to speak the complete truth.

Vikrant: Ms. Joshi, please tell the court about Mr. Ajay Sharma's contributions to your institution.

Ms. Joshi's voice grew stronger as she spoke. "Your Honour, in my twenty-two years as an educator, I have never witnessed such transformational teaching. Mr. Sharma didn't just teach children - he revolutionised how we approach early childhood education."

Vikrant: Can you be more specific?

Ms. Joshi: Over twelve years, Mr. Sharma developed what we call 'Foundation Learning' - a methodology for Jr. KG to Standard 1 that treats each child's potential as sacred. His approach was so effective that I mandated all teachers from Jr. KG through 12 to observe his classes.

Vikrant: What were the results?

Ms. Joshi: Extraordinary. Students from our school showed distinctly higher performance in later grades. Our school transformed from a struggling local institution to a nationally recognised center of excellence. We received delegations from twelve states wanting to study his methods.

Vikrant: And his influence beyond your school?

Ms. Joshi's eyes filled with tears of pride and regret. "The State Education Department invited him to conduct teacher training programs. His students won competitions at national and international levels. The man I suspended - the man I failed to protect - has actually revolutionised how this state nurtures young minds.

Cross-examination by Meena: Ms. Joshi, if he was so exceptional, why did you suspend him?

Ms. Joshi's voice broke slightly. "Because I had no alternative; I had to either suspend him or resign."

Meena: And you choose to suspend him.

Ms. Joshi: I choose both. By suspending him, I protected my school; by resigning, I listened to my inner voice.

Final Exchange Before Adjournment

As the testimony of the five women concluded, the courtroom was filled with a heavy silence. The power of their words, the consistency of their stories, and the transformation of their lives painted a picture that was difficult to ignore.

Just as Judge Kulkarni was about to rise and announce recess, Prosecutor Meena stood up:

"Your Honour, we've heard a parade of character certificates. Beautiful stories, no doubt. But let's not forget—there's a child involved. A real child. Her parents filed this complaint, not these ideal witnesses. The accused touched her. That fact must not be buried under sentiment."

The courtroom fell silent.

Vikrant rose immediately. "I was not in favour of involving a child, that is victim, but the prosecutor has forced us to do so. The child is the only witness that can say the truth. Please issue an order to produce her in front of the court."

Judge Kulkarni paused thoughtfully. "Hmm..."

"Objection. I request that the victim be excused from testifying. She is a minor. Such exposure may harm her psychologically," Meena interjected.

Vikrant's response was passionate. "Your Honour. Precedents exist where minors testified under protection. In the 2017 Goa school case, the child's clarity broke the case open. Truth does not harm—it frees."

"The child may be emotionally disturbed," Meena countered.

"Or manipulated. Let the court hear her, under surveillance, in a protected environment."

Judge Kulkarni considered for a long moment before speaking. "Very well. This court orders the victim's parents to produce the child for testimony at the next hearing. A child psychologist shall be present. We seek justice—not just for Ajay Sharma, but for truth."

The judge looked around the courtroom, his eyes taking in the faces of the witnesses who had testified, the accused man sitting quietly in the dock, and the crowded gallery of observers.

"The court has heard compelling testimony today. Six women have shared their stories of rescue, rehabilitation, and transformation. Their accounts paint a picture of a man dedicated to child protection and empowerment. However, the court must also consider the allegations that have brought us here today." He paused, allowing his words to settle.

"The testimony of these witnesses raises important questions about the nature of appropriate adult-child relationships, the difference between care and exploitation, and the role of community in protecting children. Their stories demonstrate that genuine care for children involves transparency, involvement of other adults, respect for boundaries, and focus on the child's empowerment rather than the adult's gratification."

"At the same time, the court recognizes that each case must be evaluated on its own merits. The testimony we have heard today provides context for understanding the accused's character, but it does not automatically absolve him of the current allegations."

"The court will now hear from the alleged victim. This is not a decision made lightly. The court is mindful of the potential impact on the child, and every precaution will be taken to ensure her wellbeing during the proceedings."

"The hearing of the child will be held in my chamber with only necessary personnel present. A child psychologist will be available to support the child throughout her testimony."

"Court adjourned. The next hearing will be held tomorrow at 10:00 AM."

As the judge rose and left the courtroom, the room erupted in conversation. Journalists scribbled notes, spectators discussed what they had heard, and the legal teams prepared for what would be the most crucial testimony of the trial.

Ajay Sharma sat quietly, his hands folded, looking at the five women who had stood up for him. Their eyes met his, and in that moment, there was an understanding that transcended words - a bond forged in truth and tempered by years of genuine care and respect.

The truth would soon be revealed, and justice would have its day.

Chapter 6: The Verdict

The Hour of Truth

The morning of the verdict was heavy with anticipation. Inside the courtroom, the same murmurs, the same faces, but now subdued—like the calm after a storm. The walls, once echoing with the noise of accusation, now seemed to hold their breath. Every corner of the room felt charged with electricity, as if the very air knew that destiny was about to unfold.

The gallery was packed beyond capacity. Journalists clutched their notebooks with white knuckles, their cameras ready to capture history. Parents sat rigid in their seats, torn between curiosity and guilt. Legal interns whispered among themselves, sensing they were witnessing something that would be discussed in law schools for years to come. Even the court clerks moved with unusual reverence, as if they understood the weight of the moment.

Ajay sat still, his fingers laced together, his breathing slow but heavy. He had spent many nights in judicial custody surrounded by hardened criminals, yet respected for the calmness with which he carried himself. The inmates had called him "Professor"—not mockingly, but with genuine respect. They would gather around him in the evenings, listening to his stories, seeking advice about their own children on the outside. There had been no shouting, no pleading, only stillness—like that of a teacher watching a storm from behind a closed window.

The media no longer barked at him; now they stared, curious, uncertain—like they had missed a bigger story unfolding beneath the surface. The same reporters who had once thrust microphones in his face now sat in contemplative silence, perhaps realizing that their initial narrative had been too simplistic, too eager to condemn. Some had even begun investigating his background more thoroughly, uncovering story after story of transformed lives.

Behind him, the six young women—his daughters in everything but blood—sat in a row, their faces a mixture of anxiety and determination. Asha clutched a small notebook; the same one he had given her years ago. Bhavna's hands trembled slightly, but her eyes remained fixed on the judge's bench. Chitra sat with the posture of someone who had faced injustice before and refused to bow to it. Devika's lips moved silently, perhaps offering a prayer or rehearsing words of support. Fatima held a folded piece of paper—a poem she had written the night before, titled "Truth Unveiled."

Nandini sat beside them, her presence a statement in itself. She had faced criticism for standing by her ex-husband, with some calling her naive, others suggesting she was seeking attention. But she had weathered it all with grace, knowing that truth had its own timeline, its own way of emerging from the shadows.

Pallavi, now six, sat with the composure of someone far beyond her years. The ordeal had aged her, but it had also strengthened her resolve. Despite her tender age, she had drawn pictures for her father, written simple letters in her careful handwriting, and spoken to anyone who would listen about the father who had given her life meaning.

Justice Rajendra Kulkarni entered the room with a deliberate pace. His eyes scanned the courtroom as if weighing each soul present. The judge looked older than he had at the beginning of the trial, as if the weight of the case had pressed down on him personally. His usual confident stride seemed more measured, more thoughtful. He had spent sleepless nights reviewing testimony, consulting legal precedents, and grappling with the awesome responsibility of determining an innocent man's fate.

Justice Kulkarni turned to the defence bench. The gesture was unexpected, and it sent a ripple of anticipation through the courtroom.

"I've spent hours reading depositions," he said, his voice firm but tinged with something deeper—something that trembled between empathy and duty. "But I could not overlook the pain in the eyes of the young girls who spoke for the accused." His voice carried the weight of someone who had seen too much suffering, too much injustice, but who still believed in the power of truth to set things right.

Vikrant stood and nodded, sensing the significance of the moment. The defence lawyer had aged during the trial as well, his initial confidence replaced by something deeper—a profound respect for the man he was defending and the lives that had been touched by his compassion.

Justice Kulkarni paused, visibly moved. Even the court stenographer had stopped typing, her fingers frozen above the keys. The silence in the room was not just stillness—it was reverence. It was the kind of silence that falls when people sense they are witnessing something sacred, something that transcends the mere mechanics of legal proceedings.

"This court is not here to validate emotions alone," the Judge finally said, clearing his throat, "But when humanity meets evidence, when character speaks louder than accusation, when truth emerges from the chorus of voices both for and against, the path forward becomes clear." He paused, looking directly at Ajay. "But the law demands certainty, not just moral conviction."

He looked down at his notes, then back up. The papers in his hands seemed to carry the weight of everything that had been said, everything that had been revealed.

"Still, I don't want to leave a single stone unturned. Let us sit with the victim, in my chamber." His voice carried both determination and compassion. "The truth deserves to be heard from the one person who has remained silent throughout this ordeal."

"Meena and Vikrant, please meet me in my room along with the victim girl her parents and Dr. Keshav Mehra- Child psychologist."

The Judge's Chamber

Inside the private chamber, the mood was intense but quiet. The room felt smaller than the courtroom, more intimate, as if secrets could be shared here that would be impossible in the public arena. The oak-panelled walls seemed to absorb sound, creating an atmosphere of confidentiality and trust.

The Judge sat across from a small girl—just six years old—nervous, fidgeting with her fingers. Her small legs barely reached the floor from the adult-sized chair, and she looked impossibly tiny in the formal setting. Her parents sat beside her, their faces etched with a mixture of protectiveness and apprehension. They had spent weeks preparing for this moment, yet now seemed unprepared for the gravity of what their daughter might say.

Meena, the public prosecutor, stood near the window, her usual confident demeanour replaced by something more vulnerable. She had built her case on the assumption that this child had been wronged, and now she faced the possibility that her assumption might crumble. Her hands clasped behind her back, she stared out at the city beyond, perhaps contemplating the implications of what might unfold.

Vikrant observed silently from a corner, his experienced eyes taking in every nuance of the child's body language, every flicker of expression that might reveal the truth. The stenographer had been asked to leave—this was to be a conversation, not a formal proceeding.

Justice Kulkarni softened his tone, transforming from the stern figure of legal authority into something more approachable, more grandfatherly. Years of dealing with children in family court had taught him how to create a safe space for young voices.

"Beta, do you know why you're here?" His voice was gentle, patient, the same tone he might use with his own grandchildren.

The little girl nodded slowly, but her eyes were wide—unsure. She looked around the room, taking in the serious faces of the adults, sensing the importance of the moment even if she couldn't fully understand it.

"Tell me honestly… did Ajay Sir ever scold you badly, touch you wrongly, say anything strange?" The judge's words were carefully chosen, simple enough for a child to understand, yet comprehensive enough to uncover any potential wrongdoing.

She looked around—at her mother, whose face was tense with anticipation, then at the tall man in the black coat, and finally back at the Judge. Her mother's eyes seemed to be sending some kind of message, but the child's attention was focused on the kind man asking the questions.

She shook her head gently and said in a soft, clear voice: "No… Ajay Sir is nice. He tells poems… and draws sun with smiley… He gave me star sticker when I read properly."

The words hung in the air like a revelation. Simple, innocent, devastating in their clarity. The child's voice carried no trace of fear, no hint of trauma, only the pure memory of positive interactions.

Justice Kulkarni leaned forward, his heart racing despite his professional composure. "Did he ever do anything that made you feel scared or bad?"

The girl frowned, thinking carefully. She understood that this was important, that the adults needed her to remember correctly. Her small brow furrowed with concentration as she searched her memory for any moment of fear or discomfort.

Then she looked up, confident now. "No, never. Ajay Sir is very good. He never shouts." Her voice grew stronger with each word, as if she was defending someone she cared about. "He always smiles. He makes funny voices when he reads stories. He helped me tie my shoelaces when I couldn't do it."

Her parents looked stunned—perhaps hearing from her daughter the words that could dismiss the case. Smita's face fainted. She couldn't figure out how to move the case forward and secure justice — not just for her daughter, but for all the children being deceived by men living double lives like Ajay."

Even Meena sighed—more in realization than regret. The prosecutor's shoulders sagged slightly as she understood that the foundation of her case was crumbling. Yet there was also relief in her expression, relief that no child had actually been harmed.

The Judge nodded slowly; his heart heavy with the weight of what he had just witnessed. "That's all, beta. Thank you." He smiled at the child, a smile that carried both sadness for the ordeal she had unknowingly been part of and joy that her innocence remained intact.

He turned to the others. "Let's go back."

"Sir, please," Smita said, her voice trembling, eyes brimming with tears.

"Something is terribly wrong. I don't know why my daughter is behaving so erratically. But I know someone who can help — a man whose granddaughter went through the same thing with Ajay. He even pulled her out of the school to protect her. Sir, I beg you, please give us justice. I've saved his number — please call him to the court."

Everyone in the chamber was stunned into silence. Justice looked up; his expression unreadable. "Alright, alright," he said slowly, "I will allow that."

Vikrant was shaken by this unexpected development, unsure

how to defend against Smita's sudden revelation. Her story had caught him off guard. Meanwhile, Meena was swept up in a new wave of hope.

Back in the Courtroom

As the courtroom doors opened, the group returned—quietly. The atmosphere had changed in their absence. The crowd seemed to sense that something significant had occurred, though they couldn't yet know what. Whispers died as the judge's party re-entered, and all eyes focused on their faces, searching for clues about what had transpired.

But as they stepped inside, the little girl looked ahead—and suddenly spotted someone. Her previous nervousness evaporated instantly, replaced by pure, unbridled joy.

Her face lit up like a sunrise, her eyes wide with delight and surprise.

"Ajay Sir!"

The words erupted from her with the force of genuine happiness. In a flash, she let go of her father's hand and ran forward with tiny steps—her arms wide, her face beaming with the kind of joy that only children can express so purely.

The courtroom held its collective breath. Cameras clicked, but their sounds seemed muffled by the magnitude of the moment. This was not testimony or evidence—this was truth in its most undeniable form.

Ajay stood stunned, his composure finally cracking. After weeks of maintaining his dignity in the face of accusations, after nights of wondering if he would ever see his students again, he was confronted with the most beautiful sight imaginable—a child running toward him with open arms and unconditional trust.

Before anyone could stop her, she had reached him and wrapped her arms around his legs, her small head barely reaching his waist. The embrace was tight, desperate, as if she was afraid, he might disappear again.

"Why you didn't come to class? We all waiting for you! My drawing is ready… I kept it for you!" Her words tumbled out in a rush, mixed with tears of joy and confusion. "Sir, our new teacher said you were sick. We all missed you, Are you better now?"

The courtroom froze. Even the guards blinked away surprise, their professional stoicism cracking in the face of such innocent emotion. A few journalists lowered their cameras in disbelief, suddenly understanding that they were witnessing something too pure, too sacred to be captured for public consumption. There was no script for this moment, no precedent that could guide them.

Ajay, overwhelmed, slowly bent down, his eyes misty, and placed a trembling hand on her shoulder. His voice, when it came, was barely above a whisper, heavy with emotion.

"I missed you too, beta." The words were simple, but they carried the weight of months of separation, of doubt, of fear that he might never again be allowed to do what he loved most—teach, guide, and nurture young minds.

There were no rehearsed words here. Just truth, pure and undeniable. The child's reaction had torn away all the complexity, all the adult fears and assumptions, revealing the simple reality of a beloved teacher and his devoted student.

Even the toughest faces in the courtroom softened. Hardened journalists wiped their eyes discreetly. Court officers looked away, struggling to maintain their professional composure. Some parents in the gallery began to cry, perhaps recognizing their own children in this moment, perhaps understanding for the first time the potential consequences of false accusations.

The six young women behind Ajay, now openly weeping, saw Constable Ramu rushing toward them. He went straight to Chitra and whispered something in her ear. Chitra then turned to Vikram and conveyed something that made Vikram's eyes widen in astonished excitement.

Justice Kulkarni watched the scene unfold and sternly said, "Order, order!"

The decision of Justice Kulkarni was by now almost evident to everyone present in the courtroom, given the confessional behaviour of Nisha, the victim. However, a pin-drop silence prevailed, followed by a wave of shock sweeping through the audience as they listened to the judge's words–

"Until we hear from the man who warned the victim's mother about Ajay, justice will remain incomplete,"

Vikrant: Your Honour, we have discovered new evidence. I would like to call Ms. Chitra to the witness stand.

Chitra (confidently)**:** Your Honour, our investigation has revealed that the complaint against the accused was fabricated. A criminal named Raju Bhai orchestrated this conspiracy out of revenge.

Everyone in the court was stunned.

Meena: Objection! This is mere speculation.

Vikrant: Your Honour, we have an eye-witness to support this claim.

Constable Ramu: Your Honour, Raju Bhai, a criminal, was seen conducting surveillance in the school area. Two constables deployed for traffic management near the school have confirmed this observation.

Chitra: Your Honour, I wish to inform the court that this case is artificial—fabricated.

Vikrant: Chitra, for the court's understanding, could you please explain the basis of this claim?

Chitra: Because Ajay Sir saved me—and several other girls, including Aditi—from a trafficking ring. The leader of that ring was Raju Bhai, who was sentenced to 20 years in prison.

(Murmurs spread across the courtroom.)

Chitra (continuing): After being released from prison, Raju Bhai was finding opportunity to take revenge on Ajay. He decided to exploit the recent incidents of inappropriate conducts of teachers in different schools and intentionally manipulated Nisha's parents to make them hypersensitive about Ajay's behaviour with his students.

Meena: Objection, Your Honour! This is all speculation.

Justice Kulkarni: Overruled. Ms. Chitra, continue.

Chitra: Thank you, your Honour, the victim's mother, Ms. Smita was misguided by Raju Bhai intentionally. He wanted to take revenge with Mr. Ajay.

Vikrant: We would like to recall Ms. Smita to the stand, Your Honour.

Smita's Honest Confession

Vikrant: Ms. Kulkarni, before filing the complaint, was there anyone who influenced you?

Smita (nervous, hesitant, then honest): Yes… a man….. a stranger…. approached me.

Vikrant (showing a photo to Smita): Is this the man who met you?

Smita: Yes.

Vikrant: What did he say?

Smita: He said, "Sister, my name is Vikas. My granddaughter, Priya… was just six years old. Just like your daughter. She used to come home from school upset every day. She'd say the teacher uncle gives her "special attention." His name is Ajay Sharma. He often calls children—especially little girls—alone

Vikram: Did he file a complaint against him?

Smita: He said that he had filed a complaint against him, but the school management had covered it up, in fact, they had threatened him instead.

He also said that Ajay had done this to many girls, especially street children, who have no support and no voice. He further claimed that he himself had spent 20 years in jail because of Ajay, having been falsely accused of trafficking.

Vikrant: And before meeting him, what were you thinking about Ajay Sir?

Smita (with an honest confession): He was a nice teacher and Nisha was his favourite student.

Vikrant: So, your decision was based solely on what that unknown man told you?

Smita (in guilt): Yes… I became overprotective, like any mother would. After hearing his stories, I truly believed my daughter was in danger. But now I realise—the stranger who met me was none other than the criminal, Raju Bhai. Sir, we are truly sorry. We withdraw our complaint. We made a grave mistake.

Smita collapsed in the witness stand. A wave of sorrow washed over her as she began to sob uncontrollably.

"This Court finds Mr. Ajay Sharma not guilty of the charges filed against him. I hereby order the police to take Raju Bhai into custody and initiate legal proceedings against him."

Ajay rushed to Smita and helped her to her feet. "Everything is going to be fine now, please don't cry." he said reassuringly.

A wave of sound followed—relieved gasps, muffled sobs, applause held back by respect for the solemnity of the moment. The verdict was not just legal vindication; it was moral restoration, the acknowledgment that goodness exists in the world and that it should be protected, not prosecuted.

Ajay closed his eyes—not in celebration, but in release. The burden that had weighed on him for months finally lifted.

An Unexpected Arrival

Then the doors to the courtroom opened again, and an unexpected figure appeared.

A dignified man entered—Abhishek Sharma, Ajay's estranged father and one of the city's most prominent industrialists. In a crisp grey suit, he walked forward with steady steps, his presence commanding immediate attention. His black BMW waited outside, but for the first he had chosen to walk inside, to be present for his son's moment of vindication. The courtroom stirred with surprise. Many recognized the successful businessman, knew of his wealth and influence, but few had connected him to the accused teacher. His presence here was more than unexpected—it was deeply meaningful.

Ajay froze, his emotions already raw from the verdict and the child's embrace. Seeing his father here, now, added another layer of complexity to an already overwhelming moment.

"I came to take my son home," Abhishek said, his voice carrying across the silent courtroom. His eyes swept the room, taking in the scene—the child still clinging to Ajay, the six young women wiping tears from their faces, the atmosphere of vindication and relief. He looked beyond Ajay, at the six girls standing proudly, and then at Pallavi and Nandini. "And his family."

The words were simple, but they carried profound meaning. This wasn't just about father and son—it was about acknowledging the extended family Ajay had created through his work, his dedication, his love.

Vikrant smiled, the stress of the trial finally lifting from his shoulders. "We'll need a mini bus," he said, his voice light with relief and humour.

Even Justice Kulkarni allowed himself a faint grin. "A dignified exit, Mr. Sharma," he said, his formal tone softening with genuine warmth.

Ajay turned to his father, his eyes searching the older man's face for understanding, for acceptance. "You really watched everything?" His voice carried years of hurt, years of feeling misunderstood and rejected.

He placed a hand on Ajay's shoulder, a gesture that bridged years of distance and misunderstanding. "Ajay, when you could give me the best consultant to build up my business, how can I not give you the best advocate to fight your battle? Come home. We have a business to run. And a country to educate."

Ajay's breath caught in his throat as he realized his father had discovered the truth—the business consultant who had transformed their family empire from struggling venture to soaring success had been Ajay's secret gift of love, his silent way of protecting the man who meant everything to him. But what made his heart swell with overwhelming emotion was his father's breath-taking response: in a gesture of profound gratitude and boundless paternal love, the old man had quietly arranged for Vikrant, the city's most formidable advocate, to champion Ajay's desperate legal battle—a father's fierce devotion answering his son's selfless sacrifice.

The words carried the promise of reconciliation, of a partnership that would combine resources with compassion, business acumen with social responsibility.

Ajay looked at his girls, his daughter, and Nandini—the family he had chosen and who had chosen him in return. Their faces glowed with happiness, with the knowledge that their faith had been vindicated, that their testimonies had mattered.

"We are coming home," he said, his voice strong with conviction and hope.

The courtroom erupted in spontaneous applause, the formal atmosphere finally giving way to pure human emotion. Justice had been served, truth had prevailed, and a good man was going home.

The Encounter

A minibus and Abhishek's car were waiting outside the courthouse. Abhishek, Pallavi, Vikrant, and the six girls boarded the bus, while Vikrant's driver followed in the car. Everyone was in high spirits, laughing and enjoying the moment—the girls teasing Vikrant playfully. A little later, Nandini and Ajay joined them as well.

Abhishek, overjoyed, decided to host a grand celebration at a five-star hotel. He made all the arrangements with a single phone call from his cell phone. He invited his family members and close friends, including Mr. Raghavan—Ajay's friend and a business consultant working with Abhishek.

Both vehicles set off toward the city. After some time, the minibus driver noticed a jeep blocking their path. The bus came to a halt. A thug stepped out of the jeep and climbed into the bus.

"Raju Bhai!" he roared in anger.

"You bitch!" Raju growled, glaring at Ajay.

"Because of you, I landed behind bars. Now it's your turn to pay."

He dragged Ajay out of the bus, and a fierce fight broke out between Raju's gang and Ajay. Seeing the chaos unfold, the rest of the passengers jumped out of the bus and rushed to Ajay's aid. The unexpected retaliation shocked Raju. The girls fought back with such ferocity; it was as if Goddess Durga herself had possessed them.

After several intense minutes, Aditi grabbed a heavy stone, rage burning in her eyes. She raised it above her head, ready to strike.

"There's a limit!" she screamed.

Ajay stopped her just in time, his voice calm but firm.

"There may be a limit to everything, Aditi—but not to patience. Don't ruin your future over this."

Somehow, Aditi managed to control herself. Ajay immediately called the police emergency number—100—and handed Raju over to the authorities.

Asha looked at the group: "This is the scoundrel who ruined Aditi's childhood."

All were shocked.

With fire in her eyes and a flushed red face, Aditi stood tall, breathing heavily. Everyone around her was trying to calm her down, and even Nandini was gradually settling herself. Slowly, as she kept repeating, "I'm alright, I'm alright," Aditi began to calm down. Then, unable to hold back any longer, she buried her head into Ajay and Nandini's embrace and burst into tears. After a while, she wiped her eyes and returned to normal.

The officer looked at Raju and smirked, "Welcome. You're now our permanent guest."

A little while later, the journey resumed, and the bus finally arrived at the hotel, where the celebrations awaited.

The Celebration

The party began. After a few joyful moments of laughter and delicious appetizers, Abhishek took the stage to introduce Ajay, Nandini, Pallavi, Vikrant, and the girls. He then announced the launch of the Jaynandini Edutech Foundation, dedicated to improving the quality of education in India.

The evening concluded on a graceful note with a heartfelt couple dance by Ajay and Nandini. A soft, emotional song played in the background, capturing the deep bond they shared.

As they swayed together on the dance floor, surrounded by their chosen family and blood relatives united at last, Ajay knew that this was more than vindication—it was validation- that love in its purest form could overcome the darkest accusations, that truth would always find a way to shine through, and that sometimes, the greatest victories come not from what we achieve, but from what we give to others.

The foundation they were launching would ensure that children like his six daughters would have opportunities, that other teachers like himself would be supported and protected, and that the cycle of love and learning would continue for generations to come.

In the end, the fire that had threatened to consume everything had only served to purify and strengthen what was already pure. Truth had triumphed, love had endured. and a family—bound not by blood but by choice, compassion, and unwavering faith—had emerged stronger than ever.

Chapter 7: Return of the Teacher

Back where he Belonged

A week later, in the morning, Ajay, Pallavi, Nandini and Abhishek stepped out of a car. The school gates of Vidya Vihar High School opened—calmer now, less guarded, as if welcoming back one of its own.

A small crowd had gathered outside, but their energy was different now. Where once there had been suspicion and judgment, now there was curiosity mixed with respect. Parents who had once whispered accusations now exchanged glances of acknowledgment. Some nodded respectfully. Some offered faint smiles. A few even looked relieved, as if a weight had been lifted from their own consciences.

Ms. Kapoor, the mother who had once pulled her child away from Ajay's vicinity, now approached hesitantly. "Sir," she said, her voice barely above a whisper, "I... I'm sorry. We should have known better." Her eyes glistened with unshed tears of regret.

Ajay placed a gentle hand on her shoulder. "We all learn from our mistakes. What matters is that we do better for our children."

Principal Vandana Joshi, who had re-joined the school after Ajay was declared not guilty, stood at the entrance, holding a letter in her hand. Her face showed a mix of formality and remorse, but also something else—hope. The past months had aged her visibly, the weight of her decision to suspend Ajay having taken its toll.

"I owe you more than an apology," she said softly, her voice trembling slightly. "The school turned away from truth when it should've stood firm. We failed you, and in doing so, we failed our children."

Ajay took the letter, his fingers steady despite the emotion of the moment. "Then let's make sure it never happens again. Let's build something stronger from this."

She handed him the formal reinstatement, but her gesture carried more weight than any official document. "We'd like you back in your old classroom. But more than that, we'd like you to help us create a better environment for all our teachers and students."

Ajay looked at the playground where children were already gathering, their faces pressed against the fence, trying to catch a glimpse of their beloved teacher. Some were jumping up and down with excitement, others were calling out his name. The pure joy on their faces was infectious.

"I never left it in my heart," he said, his voice thick with emotion. "And I never will."

Class 1-B

The bell rang, but today its chime carried a different tune—less a summons, more a celebration. Children hurried to their seats, their energy barely contained, eyes shining with anticipation. On the board, bold letters proclaimed: Welcome Back, Ajay Sir! Beneath the words bloomed a riot of chalk art—colourful flowers, beaming suns, and hearts that seemed to pulse with affection.

As Ajay entered, the children couldn't contain themselves. They leaped to their feet—this time not out of discipline, but pure, unbridled joy. Some were bouncing on their toes, others were clapping their hands, and a few were wiping away tears of happiness.

"Good morning, Sir!" they chorused, their voices ringing with such enthusiasm that teachers from neighbouring classrooms peeked in to see what was happening.

Ajay's eyes misted as he looked at their beaming faces. "Good morning, my little stars. My beautiful, brilliant little stars."

Before he could say another word, little Aarav from the front row couldn't contain himself. "Sir, we missed you so much! We drew pictures for you every day!"

"And we practiced reading because we wanted to show you how good we became!" added Priya, waving a small book in the air.

"Sir, sir!" called out Rohit, practically bouncing in his seat. "Will you tell us a story today? Please, please, please!"

Ajay chuckled; his heart full to bursting. "Yes, yes! But today, I want you to tell me a story—of something you feared and how you became brave."

The reaction was immediate and overwhelming. Every single hand shot up into the air, accompanied by excited squeals and pleas of "Me first, Sir!" "Pick me, Sir!" "I have the best story!"

Outside the classroom, Nandini watched through the half-open door, her hand pressed to her heart. Tears of joy streamed down her face as she witnessed the pure magic of a teacher reunited with his students. She turned to Abhishek Sharma, who stood beside her in his business suit, his own eyes suspiciously bright.

"He belongs here," she whispered, her voice filled with wonder.

Abhishek nodded slowly, understanding dawning in his eyes. "And yet, he belongs with me too. Perhaps... perhaps that's the beauty of it. He belongs wherever children need him."

A small crowd of teachers had gathered in the hallway, drawn by the sounds of joy emanating from the classroom. They watched in silence as Ajay moved among his students, his face radiant with happiness, his hands gesturing animatedly as he listened to their stories.

A New Chapter at Sharma Enterprises

In the weeks that followed, Ajay split his time between the chalkboard and the boardroom. Abhishek, now semi-retired, welcomed Ajay into the core team. Together, under the umbrella of the Jaynandini Edutech Foundation, they launched the Sharma Rural Ed-Tech Initiative, which aimed to build low-cost, solar-powered learning pods for underdeveloped schools across the country.

Ajay formed a core team under the leadership of Nandini, bringing together his six spiritual daughters—the six accomplished young women—and strategically assigning each of them responsibilities that perfectly aligned with their professional expertise and hard-earned experience. The team launched with ambitious time-bound targets, working with focused determination to ensure that the Rural Ed-Tech Initiative would achieve its fullest operational efficiency precisely when the foundation building reached completion and stood ready for full-fledged operation with all necessary facilities.

Ajay collaborated intensively with engineers to design child-friendly learning modules, while he personally crafted the story-based curriculum, drawing deeply from his transformative experiences of teaching beneath towering trees and conducting classes inside makeshift shelters where hope flourished despite humble surroundings. Meanwhile, Nandini and her dedicated team operated primarily from their homes, methodically employing qualified staff members, conducting comprehensive training programs, identifying and partnering with needy NGOs, cultivating relationships with individuals who could provide crucial support for their initiative, approaching organizations interested in contributing their CSR funds to this noble cause, and most importantly, making regular visits to underdeveloped and impoverished communities to carefully identify and select children whose lives could be completely transformed through their intervention.

Two and a half years had passed since the trial's conclusion. The time had been spent in careful planning, construction, and preparation for what would become the most comprehensive child welfare initiative the region had ever seen. The Jaynandini Edutech Foundation's headquarters was nearing completion—a beautiful, modern facility designed with children's needs at its heart.

Ajay's name was no longer whispered—it was now spoken at conferences, at education summits, at policy roundtables as a representative of the Jaynandini Edutech Foundation's innovative approach to rural education.

The transformation was remarkable. The man who had once been accused of harming children was now being invited to speak at international forums about child protection and education. Universities offered him Honorary doctorates. Government committees sought his input on education policy. But perhaps most meaningfully, other teachers began reaching out to him—not just for advice on curriculum, but for support when they faced their own challenges and accusations.

The Foundation Leadership Team

The foundation, now ready for its official launch through the unwavering commitment and exceptional leadership of Ajay, Nandini, and the six women, represented a dream come true for Ajay, his dedicated team, and his proud father.

Aditi Sharma, now 28, had completed her Master's in Social Work and gained extensive experience in child rehabilitation programs. She had worked with three different NGOs, building expertise that would make her invaluable as the foundation's Director of Child Rehabilitation Programs. She had married a fellow social worker and had a young daughter, but remained committed to the work that had given her life meaning.

Asha Sharma, now 31, had pursued her passion for education

and literacy, working with rural development programs across Maharashtra. Her experience in village-level education initiatives made her the perfect choice for Director of Educational Outreach. She lived with her teacher husband in a farmhouse outside Pune, from where she could easily coordinate rural programs.

Bhavna Desai, now 30, had become a licensed trauma counsellor and completed additional certifications in child psychology. Her personal experience combined with professional training made her uniquely qualified to serve as Director of Mental Health Programs. She was engaged to a fellow psychologist and planned to integrate her private practice with foundation work.

Chitra Joshi, now 29, had spent years working with anti-trafficking organizations and law enforcement agencies. Her expertise in child protection and her network of contacts across the criminal justice system made her the ideal Director of Child Protection. She remained single, fully dedicated to her mission of protecting vulnerable children.

Devika Mehta, now 28, had established herself as a formidable advocate for children's rights and had handled numerous high-profile cases. Her legal expertise and passion for justice made her the natural choice for Director of Legal Services. She had married a fellow lawyer and together they had adopted a young girl from one of her cases.

Fatima Ali, now 27, had published two books of poetry that had gained national recognition for their powerful portrayal of survival and hope. Her ability to give voice to the voiceless made her perfect for the role of Director of Creative Expression Programs. She lived with her partner, a journalist who often collaborated on stories about social justice.

The First Leadership Meeting

The foundation's conference room was spacious and bright,

with large windows overlooking the children's garden that would soon be filled with laughter and learning. Ajay sat at the table, no longer as a teacher addressing students, but as a colleague among equals. Nandini, now the foundation's Executive Director, facilitated the meeting. Pallavi, now 9 and wise beyond her years, sat quietly in the corner, working on her homework while listening to the discussions that would shape her understanding of leadership and social responsibility.

"It's incredible to see us all here like this," Nandini began, looking around the table. "Two and a half years ago, we were fighting for Ajay's freedom. Today, we're planning how to transform the lives of thousands of children."

Ajay smiled as he looked at each of the women. "You've all become exactly what I hoped you would—leaders, professionals, change-makers. But more than that, you've remained connected to the mission that brought us together."

Aditi leaned forward, her professional demeanour evident in her crisp white kurta and neatly organized notes. "The rehabilitation centre plans are ambitious. We're looking at residential facilities for 200 children initially, with expansion planned over five years."

"The mobile library program will complement that beautifully," Asha added, consulting her tablet. "We can reach children in remote areas who can't access residential programs but still need educational support."

Bhavna's voice carried the authority of someone who had seen the worst of human trauma and the best of human resilience. "Mental health services will be integrated into every program. We can't just address immediate needs—we have to focus on long-term healing."

Chitra's experience in law enforcement brought a different perspective. "Prevention is as important as intervention. We need to work with communities to identify at-risk situations before they become crisis situations."

Devika's legal mind was already thinking systematically. "We also need to consider policy advocacy. Individual cases are important, but systemic change requires us to influence legislation and implementation."

Fatima had been taking notes in the margins of a poetry notebook. "The children need to find their voices, not just survive their circumstances. Creative expression can be as healing as counselling."

As the meeting progressed, Ajay watched with amazement as these women—who had once been broken, frightened children—discussed budgets, strategies, and program expansions with the confidence of seasoned professionals. They challenged each other's ideas, proposed innovations, and planned for a future that would touch thousands more lives.

Pallavi looked up from her homework. "Can I ask something?" she said, her clear voice cutting through the professional discussion."

"Of course, beta," Ajay replied.

"You're all planning to help so many children, but what about your own families? Your own children?"

The question brought a moment of silence to the room. Then Aditi smiled, her expression softening as she thought of her young daughter. "That's exactly why we're doing this work, Pallavi. We want to create a world where all children—including our own—can grow up safe, loved, and full of possibility."

Evening at Home

That evening, Ajay and Pallavi returned to their modest apartment, the same space where they had shared their morning tea rituals and bedtime stories for years. The apartment had been modestly expanded to accommodate Pallavi's growing need for study space, but it remained fundamentally the same—a sanctuary of love and learning.

As they prepared dinner together, Pallavi asked, "Daddy, is it strange having the house so quiet now that the sisters visit less often?"

Ajay paused in his chopping of vegetables. The six women would always be his daughters in every way that mattered, but their evolution from dependent children to independent professionals had been exactly what he had hoped for. "No, beta. I'm proud. They've grown into exactly who they were meant to be. They have their own families now, their own lives, but they're still connected to us and to each other in the ways that matter most."

"Will they still come for Sunday dinners?"

"Every week," Ajay assured her. "Family isn't about living in the same house. It's about choosing to stay connected, to support each other, to work together for something bigger than ourselves."

The phone rang, interrupting their quiet moment. It was Abhishek, calling to discuss the foundation's funding strategy and timeline for the official launch. As Ajay spoke with his father about budgets and strategic planning, Pallavi continued setting the table, and somewhere across the city, six remarkable women were with their own families, planning the next day's work in their ongoing mission to heal and protect children.

The Foundation Meet

That Sunday, the entire extended family gathered at the foundation's nearly completed campus for what they called their "soft launch"—a private celebration before the public opening. The building was beautiful, designed with children's needs at its heart, but tonight it was filled with the laughter and conversation of adults who had found their purpose.

The six women arrived with their respective families. Aditi brought her husband and young daughter. Asha came with her teacher husband. Bhavna arrived with her fiancé. Chitra came alone but with updates from her latest anti-trafficking operation. Devika brought her lawyer husband and their adopted daughter. Fatima arrived with her journalist partner.

As they toured the facilities together—the bright classrooms, the art therapy rooms, the library filled with books in multiple languages, the garden where children would play and heal—Ajay felt a profound sense of completion. Not the completion of the work, which would continue for generations, but the completion of a circle that had begun with six frightened children and had grown into something beautiful and powerful.

Pallavi, now a confident nine-year-old, moved easily among the group, equally comfortable with the adults who had helped raise her and the children who would soon call this place home.

As the evening wound down and families began to return to their respective homes, the six women gathered around Ajay one more time.

"You know," Fatima said, her poet's eye taking in the scene, "two and a half years ago we were sitting in a courtroom, fighting for your freedom. Tonight, we're standing in a place that will free thousands of other children from the circumstances that once trapped us."

"The circle is complete," Chitra added, "but the story is just beginning."

Ajay looked at each of them—no longer his students, but his colleagues, his partners in the most important work of his life. "Class is back in session," he said with a smile. "And this time, we're all teachers."

As they prepared to leave, Abhishek pulled Ajay aside. "I'm proud of what you've built," the older man said, his voice thick with emotion. "Not just the foundation, but this family. These relationships. This legacy."

"It's our legacy now," Ajay replied. "All of ours."

The return of the teacher had become something much larger—the birth of a movement that would outlast any single person and touch countless lives for generations to come. The light that had been kindled in a moment of crisis had grown into a beacon that would guide lost children home for years to come.

Chapter 8: Lessons Beyond the Classroom

From Vision to Reality

The foundation was finally ready for its official launch. Under the dedicated leadership of Ajay, Nandini, and the six women, it had become a dream come true for Ajay, his team, and his father. But dreams, Ajay had learned, were only the beginning. The real test lay in transforming hope into action, vision into reality.

The grand opening had been a magnificent celebration that brought together everyone whose lives had been touched by this journey. Abhishek and Amruta Sharma sat in the front row with tears of pride in their eyes, flanked by Ajay's siblings Dhanush and Gayatri, finally understanding the true meaning of their brother's chosen path. Nandini's mother, Sarita Deshmukh, held little Pallavi's hand, her earlier scepticism replaced by profound respect for what love and determination could accomplish, while Nandini's sister Natasha sat beside them, her presence a symbol of family reconciliation and support.

The families of the six women occupied most of the second row—Bhavna with her fiancé and her proud parents who had travelled from their village, Fatima's mother and supportive uncle who had once forced her into marriage but now celebrated her achievements, while Aditi, Asha, Chitra, and Devika sat with the chosen families they had created: Aditi with her social worker husband and young daughter, Asha with her teacher husband, Devika with her lawyer husband and their adopted daughter, and Chitra accompanied by her police colleague partner. Principal Vandana Joshi and her entire staff from Vidya Vihar High School attended, witnessing the extraordinary growth of their former colleague, while hundreds of current and former students cheered from the gallery, their voices creating a symphony of hope. Nandini compered the entire program with eloquence and emotion, narrating the complete journey from the false accusations that had once threatened to destroy them to the transformative work that now stood as a beacon of hope for countless children.

"The Governor of Maharashtra and the Chief Minister jointly inaugurated the foundation, their speeches acknowledging this as a model for the entire nation. Following the inauguration, Nandini called the six women to the stage and narrated the remarkable success story of the foundation alongside their individual transformation stories.

Asha had journeyed from a starving street child to a literacy champion reaching forty villages. Bhavna evolved from a traumatized victim to a healer whose methods were now studied nationally. Chitra transformed from a trafficking victim to a protector who had rescued over two hundred children. Devika rose from family tragedy survivor to a legal advocate changing state policies. Fatima metamorphosed from a forced marriage escapee to a nationally acclaimed poet. Finally, Aditi's story showed her journey from a dying child in Raju Bhai's clutches to the foundation's Director of Child Rehabilitation Programs."

Thunder after thunder of applause erupted from the audience as each story unfolded, the crowd rising to their feet multiple times, moved to tears by the extraordinary journeys of courage and redemption, before the six women together delivered their moving vote of thanks that brought the entire auditorium to sustained applause, and the ceremony concluded with the national anthem sung by a choir of children whose lives had been transformed by the very programs they were celebrating.

Jaynandini Edutech Facing Major Crisis

Nine months after the grand opening, the Jaynandini Edutech

Foundation faced its first major crisis. The morning had started like any other—children's laughter echoing through the corridors, the aroma of breakfast drifting from the kitchen, and the soft hum of learning activities beginning in various rooms. Then the phone call came that would test everything they had built.

Nandini burst into Ajay's office, her usually composed demeanour cracked with urgency. "We have a problem. A big one."

"What's happened?" Ajay asked, immediately alert to the tension in her voice.

"The state government is launching an investigation into our funding sources. Someone has filed a complaint alleging financial irregularities." She sank into the chair across from his desk, her hands trembling slightly. "They're sending a team tomorrow."

Ajay felt his stomach drop. After everything they had survived—the false accusations, the trial, the slow rebuilding of trust—they now faced a new threat that could destroy everything they had worked for.

"Who filed the complaint?"

"We don't know yet. It came through official channels, but..." Nandini paused, choosing her words carefully. "Vikrant thinks it might be connected to some of the trafficking networks Chitra has been disrupting. This could be retaliation."

The Team in Crisis

An emergency meeting was called for that evening. The six women gathered in the conference room, their faces reflecting the gravity of the situation. The atmosphere was tense, charged with the kind of energy that comes when everything precious is suddenly at risk. Aditi was the first to speak, her voice steady despite the circumstances. Her young daughter was at home with her husband, both anxiously waiting for news. "How many children are we talking about if they shut us down?"

"Forty-three in residential care," Nandini replied. "Another hundred and twenty in our day programs. Plus, all the families we're supporting through the outreach initiatives."

Chitra's jaw tightened, her police colleague had warned her that retaliation was always a risk in their line of work. "This has to be connected to the Raigarh operation. We rescued eighteen children from that trafficking ring last month, and their leader, Anwar Bhai, swore revenge before they took him away."

"Revenge or not," Bhavna interjected, her counsellor's training evident in her measured tone. Her fiancé had driven her to the meeting, understanding the gravity of the situation. "We need to focus on what we can control. Our documentation, our processes, our ability to demonstrate the legitimacy of our work."

Fatima had been unusually quiet, her notebook open but blank. Her journalist partner had offered to help with media strategy if needed. "What about the children? How do we explain this to them without traumatizing them all over again?

"It was the question that cut to the heart of everything. These children had already been abandoned, betrayed, and disappointed by the adults who should have protected them. How could they now face the possibility of losing the one place that had become home?

Devika, ever the lawyer, was already thinking strategically. Her husband had helped her prepare legal documents throughout the evening. "We need to be completely transparent with the investigators. Open our books, show them our impact data, introduce them to the children and families we've helped. Turn this into an opportunity to showcase our work."

"And if that's not enough?" Asha asked quietly, thinking of the remote villages where her mobile libraries had become lifelines for children.

The silence that followed was heavy with unspoken fears.

The Investigation

The next morning brought a convoy of government vehicles to the foundation's gates. Three investigators, two accountants, and a social worker climbed out, their official badges and clipboards creating an atmosphere of cold bureaucracy that seemed to suck the warmth from the colourful campus.

Ajay met them at the entrance, flanked by Nandini and Vikrant. "Welcome to Jaynandini Edutech Foundation," he said, his voice calm despite the circumstances. "We're here to answer any questions you might have."

The lead investigator, a stern-faced woman named Ms. Kulkarni, barely acknowledged the greeting. "This is a formal inquiry into allegations of financial mismanagement and improper use of funds. We'll need access to all financial records, staff files, and program documentation."

"Of course," Nandini replied smoothly. "We have everything prepared for your review."

As the investigators began their work, the foundation's normal routine continued around them. Children attended classes, participated in art therapy, played in the garden. But there was an undercurrent of tension that even the youngest could sense. Some of the older children, those who had vivid memories of officials who brought bad news, watched the strangers with wary eyes.

Nine-year-old Pallavi approached one of the investigators during lunch break, her child's directness cutting through the adult complexity of the situation. "Are you here to close our school?" she asked.

Ms. Kulkarni looked down at the girl, her official mask slipping slightly. "We're here to make sure everything is being done properly."

"It is," Pallavi said with absolute certainty. "My daddy and his family work very hard to take care of us. You can ask anyone."

Voices of Truth

Over the next three days, the investigators interviewed staff, reviewed financial records, and observed programs in action. What they discovered was not the mismanagement they had expected, but a meticulously run organization where every rupee could be accounted for and every decision was made with the children's welfare as the primary consideration. But it was the children themselves who provided the most compelling testimony.

Rahim, a ten-year-old who had been rescued from a glass factory where he had worked twelve-hour days, told the investigators how he was learning to read and write for the first time. "Before I came here, I thought I was stupid," he said simply. "Now I know I just needed someone to teach me."

Meera, twelve years old and recovered from severe malnutrition, showed them the vegetable garden she was helping to maintain. "We grow our own food here," she explained proudly. "And we learn about nutrition and taking care of ourselves."

Arjun, eight years old and formerly mute from trauma, sang a song he had learned in music therapy, his voice clear and strong as it filled the room.

One by one, the children shared their stories—not just of rescue, but of transformation. They spoke of dreams they had developed, skills they had learned, and most importantly, of feeling safe and valued for the first time in their lives.

The Breakthrough

On the third day, as Ms. Kulkarni was reviewing the

foundation's educational outcomes data, she came across something that made her pause. The literacy rates, the psychological assessment scores, the health improvements—the numbers told an extraordinary story of systematic transformation.

"These results," she said to Ajay during their final meeting, they're remarkable. In my fifteen years of investigating child welfare organizations, I've never seen data like this." "The children are remarkable," Ajay replied. "We just provide them with what every child deserves—safety, love, and opportunity."

Ms. Kulkarni set down her pen and looked directly at him. "Mr. Sharma, I came here expecting to find financial irregularities and program failures. Instead, I've found what might be the most effective child welfare operation in the state."

She paused, her official demeanour softening slightly. "I also discovered something else. The complaint against you was filed by someone using false credentials. We believe it was indeed retaliation for your anti-trafficking work."

Vindication and Growth

The investigators' final report not only cleared the foundation of any wrongdoing but recommended it as a model for other organizations. The state government, impressed by the outcomes and the rigorous management practices, offered additional funding for expansion.

But the real vindication came from an unexpected source. A week after the investigation concluded, a letter arrived addressed to Ajay in beautiful handwriting. It was from Ravi, one of his former students from Vidya Vihar High School, who had heard about the investigation and wanted to show his support.

"Dear Ajay Sir," the letter read, "I heard some people were saying bad things about your foundation. I wanted you to know that you saved my life when you were my teacher. Before I met you, I thought I was not good at anything. Now I have dreams and I am doing well in my studies. Thank you for believing in me when no one else did."

Similar letters began arriving from children, families, former students, and even teachers at other schools who had heard about the investigation and wanted to show their support. The foundation's mailbox overflowed with testimonials to the impact of their work, both past and present.

The six women felt the support not just professionally but personally. Aditi's husband took time off work to help with crisis management. Asha's teacher husband organized support from his school community. Bhavna's fiancé and parents drove down to offer moral support. Chitra's police colleague provided informal security during the tense investigation period. Devika's husband offered legal counsel, while Fatima's journalist partner helped manage media inquiries.

The Ripple Effect Begins

News of the investigation's positive outcome spread through the child welfare community like wildfire. Organizations from other states began reaching out, asking for guidance on implementing similar programs. The foundation suddenly found itself at the centre of a movement it had never intended to lead.

Aditi fielded calls from NGOs in Karnataka and Tamil Nadu who wanted to adapt their rehabilitation model. Asha received requests from education departments in three states interested in her literacy programs. Chitra was invited to train law enforcement officers across the region.

"We've created something bigger than we realized," Nandini observed during a team meeting. "The question is: are we ready for what comes next?"

It was Pallavi who provided the answer. During dinner one evening, she looked up from her homework and said, "Daddy, in my English class today, we learned about seeds. The teacher said that some seeds need to be scattered by the wind to grow in new places."

Ajay smiled at his daughter's wisdom. "What do you think that means for us, beta?" "I think it means our love is ready to travel to new places," she said simply. "But it will always grow back to where it started."

Looking Forward

As the first year of full operation approached, the foundation had proven its worth, survived its first major crisis, and established itself as a model for others to follow. From a single facility serving fifty children, it had begun to inspire a network of organizations across multiple states who wanted to replicate their approach. The Foundation decided to appoint a permanent chartered accountant to avoid the risk of non-compliance and subsequent interference from the concerned authorities.

The six women had evolved from grateful former students to recognized leaders in their fields. Their expertise was sought by universities, government committees, and organizations nationwide. Yet they remained grounded in the daily work of healing and transformation, understanding that true impact was measured not in awards or recognition but in the changed lives of individual children.

Their personal relationships had been tested and strengthened by the demands of their work. They had learned to balance professional ambition with personal fulfilment, to maintain their commitment to the mission while nurturing their own families and partnerships.

But perhaps most importantly, the foundation had maintained the heart that had always driven its work—the understanding that every child deserves to be seen, valued, and given the opportunity to discover their own potential.

The Promise of Tomorrow

As Ajay tucked Pallavi into bed one evening, she surprised him with a question that showed how much she had grown during this transformative year. "Daddy, do you think the children we help today will help other children someday?" He sat on the edge of her bed, struck by the wisdom in her young voice. "What do you think, beta?" "I think they will," she said confidently. "Because that's what love does. It keeps going from person to person, making everyone stronger."

"You know, I've been thinking about writing down some of our stories," she continued thoughtfully. "Maybe someday people will want to read about how everything began, how the truth came out, how love won." Ajay's heart swelled with pride and amazement. At just nine years old, his daughter was already thinking like a storyteller, already understanding that their experiences had value beyond their immediate impact. "That's a beautiful idea, beta. What would you call such a book?" She was quiet for a moment, her young mind working through possibilities. "Maybe... 'The Touch of Truth'? Because that's what you gave everyone—the truth about what love can do."

As he kissed her goodnight and turned off the light, Ajay reflected on the truth of her words. They weren't just running programs or providing services—they were planting seeds of love and resilience that would bloom in ways they might never see but would certainly feel.

The work was far from over. But as he looked out at the lights of the city beyond their window, Ajay felt a deep sense of satisfaction. They had built something that would outlast any of them individually.

Chapter 9: A Gathering of Hope

A Decade of Transformation

Ten years had transformed everything. The Jaynandini Edutech Foundation now operated across twelve states with forty-seven centres serving over 8,000 children annually. The small building in Pune had become the headquarters of a movement that had touched nearly 50,000 lives.

Aditi's rehabilitation programs were now mandatory training for all child welfare officers in Maharashtra. Asha's mobile libraries reached 400 villages, with literacy rates improving by 60% in target areas. Bhavna's healing circles were integrated into 200 schools nationwide. Chitra's anti-trafficking protocols had been adopted by five state governments, leading to the rescue of over 3,000 children. Devika's legal clinic had won landmark cases that changed national child protection laws. Fatima's poetry books were taught in universities as examples of trauma-informed literature.

The six women, now in their early forties, had become national figures. Each led their specialized divisions while remaining united by their shared history and purpose.

The Anniversary Preparations

For six months, the entire team had worked tirelessly preparing for the tenth anniversary celebration. The foundation's modest auditorium could no longer accommodate the response they had received. Instead, they booked the sprawling Shivaji Ground in Pune—he same venue where great leaders had once addressed the nation.

Pallavi, now nineteen and pursuing psychology and creative writing at Pune University, had taken charge of coordinating with publishers, media houses, and logistics teams. Her days began at 5 AM, managing everything from stage design to guest accommodations. The six women worked around the clock—Aditi coordinating with beneficiaries across twelve states, Asha organizing cultural performances by children from 400 villages, Bhavna managing counselling support for emotional moments, Chitra ensuring security protocols, Devika handling legal clearances and permissions, and Fatima crafting the narrative flow of the entire program.

Nandini, now the foundation's CEO, supervised every detail while preparing for what would be the most important address of her career. Ajay watched with amazement as his daughter and the women who had once been frightened children orchestrated an event that would host over 20,000 people.

The Magnificent Gathering

On the morning of February 15th, Shivaji Ground buzzed with unprecedented energy. Where 2,000 people had attended the foundation's opening, today over 20,000 filled the massive ground. The crowd included the Prime Minister of India, three Chief Ministers, education ministers from fifteen states, international delegates from twelve countries, and thousands of beneficiaries who had travelled from across the nation.

Giant screens displayed the foundation's journey through photographs and videos. Former street children, now engineers and teachers, mingled with ministers and academics. Trafficking survivors who had become advocates shared their experiences with international researchers. The transformation was visible in every face, every conversation, every moment of recognition and pride.

The stage, designed like a lotus blooming from water, symbolized how beauty could emerge from the murkiest circumstances. Banners in twelve languages proclaimed the foundation's motto: "Every Child Deserves to Bloom."

Nandini's Masterful Compering

As the program began, Nandini took the stage with the confidence of someone who had witnessed and guided every step of this extraordinary journey. Her voice, clear and strong, carried across the vast ground through state-of-the-art sound systems.

"Ten years ago, 2,000 people gathered to witness the birth of a dream," she began, her words reaching every corner of the massive gathering. "Today, 20,000 hearts beat together to celebrate how that dream became a movement that has transformed 50,000 lives."

She unfolded the foundation's growth like a masterfully written story. Starting with six frightened children in a small room, she narrated how the foundation had grown step by step, year by year, touching milestones that once seemed impossible. From the first mobile library serving three villages to reaching 400 communities. From one healing circle to 200 schools. From rescuing dozens to saving thousands.

"Each number represents not a statistic, but a story. Not a case file, but a child who learned to dream again," Nandini's voice resonated with emotion as she presented a decade of systematic transformation.

Voices of Change

The Chief Ministers spoke of how the foundation's model had transformed child protection in their states. Dr. Raja Kumbhar, now Director of Child Welfare in Delhi, announced: "The Jaynandini Edutech model has significantly reduced child trafficking in participating districts. This foundation has rewritten the textbook on child protection."

International delegates announced partnerships that would take the foundation's model to Nepal, Bangladesh, Kenya, and three other African countries.

The Prime Minister delivered the keynote address, praising the foundation as "a beacon of hope that has shown the world what dedicated service can achieve." He then made an unexpected announcement that sent ripples of excitement through the crowd: "Today, I am proud to announce that we are nominating Shri Ajay Sharma and Smt. Nandini Sharma for the Nobel Peace Prize, recognizing their extraordinary partnership in child rehabilitation and transformation that has created a revolutionary model for healing society's most vulnerable members."

The applause was so prolonged that it continued for more than five minutes, and the PM himself had to urge the audience to settle down.

The Moment of Truth

After all the distinguished guests had spoken, Nandini returned to the stage for the most anticipated moment of the day. The massive crowd fell silent as she adjusted the microphone and looked directly at Ajay, who sat in the front row with tears of pride in his eyes.

"There is someone among us today who has a very special gift for the man who started this journey," Nandini announced, her voice thick with emotion. "Ten years ago, a nine-year-old girl told her father she wanted to write a book about their story. Today, that girl has kept her promise."

Pallavi walked onto the stage, carrying a beautifully bound book. She was no longer the shy child who had once hidden behind Ajay's legs, but a confident young woman whose presence commanded the attention of 20,000 people.

"This book is called **The Touch of Truth**" Pallavi's clear voice carried across the ground. "It's the story of how one man's faith in children changed not just our lives, but thousands of others. She raised the book and continued, "This is not about the man who stood in court. This is about the man who stood behind others, and never asked to be seen."

This is a story about seven daughters—six plus me—who learned that healing is possible. It's about how family isn't about blood, but about belonging. It's about how love becomes unstoppable when it touches truth, and about a father who chose love over convenience, and courage over comfort. Ultimately, it's about how one touch of truth can light up the world.

The crowd again erupted in sustained applause that lasted longer than before. Twenty thousand people rose to their feet as Pallavi walked to her father and placed the book in his hands.

Ajay walked onto the stage, accepting the book with trembling hands. For a moment, the father and daughter simply looked at each other—he seeing the confident young woman she had become, she seeing the man whose love had made everything possible. The crowd watched in reverent silence as Ajay opened the book to the dedication page.

"To my Papa, who taught me that the greatest truth is love, and the greatest love is truth. And to all the children who are still waiting to be seen—your time is coming."

With the afternoon sun setting over Pune and the applause settling down, the crowd slowly began to disperse. Pallavi remained on stage, watching the scene below with wonder. In ten years, her father's touch of truth had indeed become a movement that would outlive them all. "The story ends here," she whispered to herself, then smiled and corrected: "No, it begins again. It begins with every child who learns they matter, with every adult who chooses to see rather than look away."

–The End--

9 789334 406757

Printed at Repro India Ltd.